Ed and Linda,

My prayer is you will
discover new things about
yourselves from this book

Bless you,
Dave S

Ephesians
2:10

INSPIRATION
from a
MASTERPIECE
A WORK OF ART

D.C. Schorno

ISBN 978-1-63630-726-8 (Paperback)
ISBN 978-1-63885-255-1 (Hardcover)
ISBN 978-1-63630-727-5 (Digital)

Although the author and publisher have made every effort to ensure that the information in this book was correct at press time, the author and publisher do not assume and hereby disclaim any liability to any party for any loss, damage, or disruption caused by errors or omissions, whether such errors or omissions result from negligence, accident, or any other cause.

Note: All illustrations in this book were created by the author; he made the decision to resurrect his artistic ability (gift) which he has not embraced since childhood. His hope is that everyone who reads this book will also find joy in his artwork.

Covenant Books, Inc.
11661 Hwy 707
Murrells Inlet, SC 29576
www.covenantbooks.com

Are you invented or created? We all search for meaning and purpose in life in our search for significance. We desire a sense of gratification from our vocation, our education, or our marriages, but do we know what we really need, or who or what we are, oftentimes we don't. In this book, I hope to inspire and challenge people, to search to discover who they truly are created to be according to God's design.

CONTENTS

FOREWORD

So if you are reading this foreword, then my first book has made it to a publisher. Never in my wildest dreams would I ever believed that one day, from all the vocations and trades I've worked during my life, I would be an author or writer.

In school, I despised language arts, I dreaded English class; therefore, I don't know how to express to you how astonished and perplexed this project has made me feel. I believe a lot of the energy it took for me to comprise and put this book together stems from the frustration residing in my mind regarding my life experiences and the inability to understand it all. Nevertheless, these circumstances gave me inspiration and motivation to put it on paper and boy did I; there has never been a moment in my life I can remember in which I was able to write my thoughts in a notebook. My ability to write, in my opinion, is less than sufficient to be a successful author; however, I must put forward the effort, for I believe the Lord wants me to tell my story for it may very well encourage the readers to take a closer examination of the direction they may be heading. They may need to realign it to the genuine one created for them by God. I have tried to not make this book another self-help purpose searching manual with the same old thoughts and popular principles but one that will help locate your person and see the being you were created to be, a work of art, one of a kind.

ACKNOWLEDGMENTS

First and foremost, credit goes to my God, my Maker and Savior, for his creativity and passion, to give us life, life in abundance, for revealing himself in such provocative and marvelous ways. Once again, words are insufficient to communicate my gratitude.

Thanks goes to my wife, Janet, for all those dark cold rainy winter nights watching me sit at my computer and putting yourself second. You never once complained about receiving little to no attention from me in the evenings after a long day working at the office. I would have never been able to succeed at this endeavor without your love and support. You are my soul mate. I love you.

Also, I give thanks to Debbie Allen for being a great boss and friend, for nurturing me along my career for the last twenty years, mentoring me, teaching me, supporting me, and being my friend. You are an inspiration to all whom you touch. I also want to give thanks to Joe Sneva for inspiring me to write this book, to share my thoughts and struggles with the world.

There are many other souls to mention who impacted my existence, including Pastor Billy Graham, Pastor Rick Warren, Reverend Arie Poot, Pastor Ron Schenk, Dr. Dallas Willard, Coach Spud Walley, Coach Ed Simons, Coach Al Harris, Coach Brian Riggins, Coach Ron John, Coach Mark Jury, Coach Hugh Galbraith, and Mr. Williamson. I gained most of my life philosophy from these great role models. Remarkably, these men may have hoped to make a difference or maybe not, but they did. These mostly ordinary men with no second thoughts about the impact their lives might make on our culture and our children, rather emulating good, wholesome moral values to young men, never once questioning, "Is this my duty?" but out of love and sacrificial time and effort to mentor young men like myself. I am thankful to all these "heroes" beyond belief. And many thanks go to Covenant Books for all their support and assistance helping me along this process. They have been so very professional and caring with much guidance.

I dedicate this book to all those who endeavor to discover their
true self and see themselves as God intended them to be seen.

INSPIRATION
from a
MASTERPIECE

A WORK OF ART

Are you invented?

Are you created?

Are you something?

Are you nothing?

What are you?

Who are you?

INTRODUCTION

What would be your first reaction to the notion that from the point of conception, you knew exactly what you were created for? Or to put it in a different perspective, God preprogrammed your self-awareness mechanism to know exactly what your life purpose or purposes were going to be. Or to put it in another light, he revealed to you every talent, skill, gift awareness, special gifts, and unique gifts, etc. Would this arrangement be profitable? Likely not, but if you're like me or many other people in the world today or in the past that share this thought you may be intrigued with it.

I still struggle, what about my life experience, or yours? I often wonder how God came up with the story of my life or everyone else's lives for that matter. What am I supposed to do with it? How am I going to make a difference, or leave a lasting legacy? It has always been obvious to me that my contributions always look so small and insignificant. What could I do to make a lasting impact on this generation and many more souls that will come after me and what will be my stamp on this earth? My frustration has continued for many years and I was close to giving up. I prayed to God for clarity, I fasted, I became more involved in our church, asked people I knew who were very holy people in my opinion; but I still was left unsettled.

So finally I was struck with a vision and an answer: write a book. At first, that notion to me and my pea-sized brain seemed ridiculous; preposterous—no way I can't do that! When I was in school I could barely make a C in English class or language arts or writing for that matter, mostly D's. But God in all his loving greatness can pull off anything. He is patient and wanting his children to be fruitful and bear fruit that will last, he put the necessary resources he knew I needed within my reach, praise the Lord!

So now I was left with the question, what kind of book should I write? I have an astounding record in my memory bank of lessons that my life journey has given to me according to God's grace and mercy. I thought maybe I should share some of them. Somewhat of a life biography, but I also want to inspire people and motivate them by sharing some stories of people from the past and stories of people that shared moments in time with me.

So my first concern about writing a book is not the fact that I don't have the slightest clue as to where do I begin, but my real concern is not making money or financial gain from the proceeds. Someone will benefit from the copyrights for sure, and just that fact disturbs me somewhat. My second concern is my lack of writing skills in language arts. But praise God for the resources that he has blessed me with. Whether you find value in this book or not, I'm hoping you will be inspired to step beyond your fears and doubts and "ask, seek, and knock" (Matthew 7:7–8).

DO IT NOW, WHAT
ABOUT THESE? GOD
IS IN CONTROL

So let's get started. Now that I am in my late fifties, I seem to have more questions than answers to many of life's circumstances. When I was in my thirties and forties, I was, to some degree, in circumspection, coasting. I thought maybe I had reached a pinnacle of some sort regarding my holiness and the wisdom that God had given to me, which is a gift. At times, I was not sure of myself or completely certain. I was convinced there should be more significance to my existence. I was waiting for God to tell me without a doubt unequivocally what to do with the rest of my life, all the rest of my days until I take my last breath at death and that would settle it. I often think about Rocky Balboa, the boxer in the movie *Rocky*. Some of you might remember the fourth movie *Rocky 4* he is fighting a big Russian boxer who killed his friend, "Apollo Creed," in a boxing match earlier in the movie. Rocky's coach tells him, "You know what you have to do, Rock, you have to knock him out, now do it, do it now!" There is no question about this instruction, direct and to the point, that's what I was searching for.

Here is some theology, thesis statement, X is good = X is willed by God.

The Bible teaches good = intrinsic good, "Sunum-bonum" (Latin). Man's highest good is the will of God as moral precept. X is right = X is willed by God. My highest good "Sunum-Bonum." Nothing comes from nothing. As a reminder that hard work is always required in order to achieve something. This is just an example from one of my theology professors, I thought would be helpful.

Feelings are so deceptive; emotions are very dishonest. Sensuality looks as though it is "perfecto" of all. This is a huge mountain to climb and conquer. The line between love and lust is so blurred one can have little success discerning one from the other. These are some elements to be considered when making choices for one's life.

Uniqueness, gifts of the spirit, fingerprints, DNA, twin siblings, the complexity of the human eye, personalities. These are just a few things that determine our uniqueness. How do I discover my uniqueness, myself, my person, my being? I hear evangelists and new-generation pastors on television talk and speak about it all the time. Then I hear pastors and leaders that say there is no such thing for a Christian to search for. So this is my dilemma. Would a loving God give me a distinct set of fingerprints and DNA that I cannot completely use for his glory as such, but if I received a gift, maybe a talent, or skill, or special insight, or ability, a physical or intellectual gift, would these gifts not give him much greater glory and satisfaction in the process of my existence? So is it profitable for myself to wrestle with these complexities of thought and principles?

I have been blessed enough to serve in many capacities in the organization called the church or body of Christ. I've served in leadership as an elder and a trustee, as well as a moderator. I was an officer on the Pastors Advisory board and nominating committee and have served and still serve as a deacon. I have been a Sunday school teacher for children and grade school, middle school and some teens as well. I also have taught adult classes. I have served in these positions and performed all that was required of them in their respected capacities. But I have never served as a pastor or missionary. Some years ago I thought maybe I would try the missionary field just short term. But I have some lifelong health issues to contend with, and I need special treatment and nutritional support as well. So I asked myself what is special about me. What can I do to leave a legacy of significance in the church of Jesus? How am I unique? The famous pastor of Lakewood Church in Houston, Texas, Joel Osteen prides himself with the statement, "You need to fulfill your destiny." Jesus says in Matthew 7:7–11, "Ask and it will be given to you; seek and you will find; knock and the door will be opened to you." So in the eyes of this poor sinful beggar, if my Heavenly Father chooses to set me apart solely on the uniqueness of my fingerprints or DNA pattern that I possess, why not give me something of greater significance that would bring him tremendous glory and wonderful joy? Is it possible that he may not be the personal relational being we thought he was all along? "For everyone who ask receives; he who seeks finds; and to him who knocks the door will be opened. Which of you, if your son asks for bread, will give him a stone? Or if he asks for a fish, will give him a snake? If you, then, though you are evil, know how to give good gifts to your children, how much more will your Father in heaven give good gifts to those who ask him!" Matthew 7:8–11.

In Romans 12:6–21 Paul speaks of the gifts God has generously given to us as members of his body, "The body of Jesus Christ." Paul gives us instruction on how to use them in everyday life. All gifts are unselfish in nature. For example, teaching is for the benefit of the student. The teacher will not always find fulfillment in teaching will they? What about the other gifts? According to the Apostle Paul generosity, hospitality, forgiveness, and compassion should be the guide post of our lives. All the gifts mentioned in verses 6 through 8 are unselfish in content and practicing them will not always give us validation or satisfaction, but it does align us with the will of God. It accomplishes complete perfect obedience, which God will honor and bless.

I will make a concerted effort to be both objective and subjective throughout each issue we discuss. We are partners with God. Like it or not, God partners himself with us to do his work or will on earth. We can say that this is a very special and honorable act of God. This is an awe-inspiring thought, a great responsibility, for us to do the work of God on earth, and him to be our partner. We should commit ourselves to whatever, wherever, whenever his will be done! Amen! We are Christ's body on earth.

I always have had the hope and confidence that I would find exactly what God created me for at some point in my life journey. I am now approaching sixty years of age, and I still have no more certainty about my place in time and history. Does this searching that I do make any difference? Can it change God's providence? Can it affect his sovereignty? I know of a woman who fell in love and married a handsome man. They had two wonderful little boys. The authorities think he murdered her but could not prove it. He explained that she left him and the boys one day, just left and abandoned him and the two little boys. Then when the truth was close to being revealed he killed the two little boys and then he killed himself. I often wonder about her and those little boys about their lives. How could this be their destiny? What good purpose could all this tragedy bring forth? Why were those little boys even born? They lived to be three and five years old, and then be exterminated by their own father? What was this purpose? What was this family given life for? Was it God's providence? How? Why was it her destiny to marry this monster? Why did God allow this? What special purpose did she have? What was her unique gift? Did she accomplish the purpose God gave her life for? Or is she just one of trillions of lost souls doomed to destruction living no more than the short thirty or forty years granted to her? How did this tragedy glorify the Lord? It's a mystery why she would be destined or willed to live on this sinful planet, according to or in alignment with God's providence. We do not know the plans of God; this is a fact that frustrates me.

I could not explain this situation to anyone. Suppose a person who does not know Jesus Christ as their savior. How do I ascertain the reasoning that comes with it? So a non-believer is questioning me about this situation. What do I say? I do not have an answer. Even though, my theology is not that of a beginner. But all in all, what should my response be? Should I say well we have to have faith? Faith that God knows what he is doing? "Love one another," "be hopeful," "be patient." "Show mercy." "Be joyful." Mourn with those who mourn." "Laugh with those who laugh." "Cry with those who cry." These are words that Jesus spoke, words that the Apostle Paul spoke, words that the Apostle Peter spoke. "Rejoice with those who rejoice."

And what about those children who are never born, or the children that have a terminal illness? They may not live to see their fifth birthday. What about their purpose, their uniqueness, their gifts, their destiny? This can be complicated to evaluate and determine a conclusion to these life experiences. So I will try to speak in hypothetical terms. Would it be safe to conclude that these sick children are ill solely for giving purpose to those who are treating them and taking care of them hypothetically speaking? Though these children are cursed with these diseases due to a fallen world, they are still able to have purpose. These conditions are used by a perfect loving God to accomplish his good and perfect will in others' lives.

JOB

So I often examine the story of Job. God's goodness is not dependent upon my own actions. I am a sinful human being who has limited understanding. I know Job struggled with this truth. I also want to analyze the intentions of God in this story. The first issue I would like to discuss has to do with God's conversation with Satan. The agreement that the Lord had with Satan seems more like a wager to me. The only difference is, God didn't bet anything tangible. Was God hoping that Job's true holiness and obedience through total destruction of his household somehow, would bring Satan to a repentant heart? God is or is not omnipotent and omniscience? If God is all knowing then God would have foreknowledge that Satan would not relent or repent no matter how obedient Job would be or how much Job would suffer from his losses.

It is clear that all of Job's household, which is his first household, was destined for destruction. God willed that, or a better explanation would be that it was God's permissive will to allow Satan to take and destroy all of Job's household. God lifted the fence that protected his existence, which Satan referred to at the beginning of their conversation. Whatever it was; as far as Job's intentions of his heart it didn't matter, Job was a righteous man and in this situation that did not matter. Destiny and fate awaited his household. His children his servants, all his livestock it was all taken away, Job was ruined.

Why would all this happen? So was this the purpose for all who lived within Job's household, for those people to be born only to be killed to prove a point to Satan? Do you think these souls would want to be born if they were given the knowledge about their coming fate beforehand? About their unique purpose, which that is what it was a unique purpose. They were born to be destined to die in this manner in this moment in time according to God's sovereign plan. Maybe, Job reasoned why did my children have to die? Or let's go a little further, what if we had foreknowledge of our children before they were born. What if we knew what they would become as adults? What if they were gay or lesbian or maybe they became murderers or child molesters or just evil. Knowing their character well before they were born, would this knowledge have an impact on our decision to procreate or not? But Job, just like us doubted God's goodness in his time of great sorrow and suffering and mourning though he made a great effort to draw closer to the Lord. We should put into practice just like Job, the principles that keep us close to God, in times of great joy and gladness and times of great sorrow and suffering.

So I return to the same question I started with, will God not explain to me somewhere on the plane of my existence the uniqueness of my being and my destiny before I wake up one day and hear the words, "Well done, good and faithful servant!" It feels like a game show quiz. I certainly hope not! Jesus told Peter the exact events that would take place in Peter's life. Jesus told him the exact way he would die, and not just Peter but all the disciples.

I know that this is the appointed time, the time of God's favor, the time of salvation, and we have the instructions in Matthew 28:16–20. I still have that feeling in my gut, which tells me to keep searching because you haven't found it yet. You haven't reached the end of the road yet. You are not there yet. You have not blossomed yet, you have not found that perfect spot that fits your shape yet.

We cannot and we should not challenge God when we don't fully understand what comes to pass around us, when circumstances don't align with our hopes, and dreams, and visions. Especially when it comes to our moral and spiritual standards, or our own rationality, how we perceive life and lives. We cannot question the Almighty, the maker of heaven and earth! "The Great I Am." For God is neither obligated nor indebted to give us anything no explanations; in fact who are we, mortal men to talk back to God? We must accept it all as our lot in life, and to live it to God's fullest glory! The greatest wise man that ever lived put it this way. "King Solomon."

"Go eat your food with gladness and drink your wine with a joyful heart, for it is now that God favors what you do. Always be clothed in white and always anoint your head with oil" (Ecclesiastes 9:7–8). Solomon says to enjoy your life and worship the Lord in all you do in these verses. And he goes on to say, "Enjoy life with your wife whom you love all the days of this meaningless life that God has given to you under the sun all your meaningless days, for this is your lot in life and in your toilsome labor under the sun." Now I know that Solomon was a little cynical and disillusioned when he wrote these verses but they ring true at times. So I'm still pondering the question about destiny, if God has foreknowledge for when he gives life to a person or persons and they choose to live life for themselves indulging in all pleasures, and they die in their sins not listening to the spirits call to repentance, they never turn to the Lord, and God knowing from before they were born, they would live all their days in sin and never turn their attention to the living God. God having foreknowledge, would still let them live? Why? They serve no purpose for God's glory? But God showing great love and mercy gives them life. I'm trying to be objective we know from scripture Jesus declared, "Many are called but few are chosen" (Matthew 22:14). Jesus also said, "Enter through the narrow gate, for wide and broad is the road that leads to destruction, and many enter through it. But small is the gate and narrow the road that leads to life, and only a few find it" (Matthew 7:13–14).

"Whatever your hands find to do, do it with all you're might for in the grave where you are going there is neither working or planning nor knowledge nor wisdom" (Ecclesiastes 9:9–10).

For when we replace the wisdom of this world with the wisdom of God, it will be a radical change. We begin to comprehend who God is and what he is doing. We will not always understand every last detail, for we are being built up into a holy priesthood prepared for eternity. We cannot receive all the information we desire, for it would overwhelm our minds; we are unable to process the deep things of God. But God in his providence foreknows all our actions and spoon feeds us little by little. So the potter has the right to use the clay for whatever purposes he so chooses, some for places of honor, and some for common uses. God is, "Elohim" (Mighty Creator) Hebrew, what right does the created have, to talk back to the creator, "God?" This is a profound mystery that I am unable to process. God asked Job where he was when God created the universe. God asked him if he could fathom all the great mysteries of the galaxies, the animal kingdom, and the insects and so on, and Job was humbled.

I have been suffering from a disease since the age of six years old; it is progressing and becoming somewhat debilitating at times. I can never fully understand why God chose to let me exist virtually my whole life suffering from it. I've come to some conclusions but no solid reasons. One thing I do know for sure is, continual suffering for long periods of time will shake your faith. When I was a child I was teased a lot and made fun of mostly from my disease. I didn't want to go to school. I began to have a low self-esteem and no confidence. I often thought to myself what does this mean? What plan does God have in mind for me? Why did he let me experience these cruel struggles? I realized after sometime that I can use these negative elements to glorify God and further his kingdom. Yes, so I became an inspirer to people. I lift them up when they are down. I give them hope. I let them know how much God loves them and wants a relationship with them. I encourage them, telling them that they are doing a great job whatever they are doing. I let them know how special and important they are to the Lord. I tell them they are a blessing to everyone around them, I tell them to never give up, keep running the race, keep climbing the mountain, keep fighting to be holy, God is using you for a special unique purpose and he wants to bless you immensely. I urge them to not be frightened or hesitant, just take that first step and then another, and before long, you will be walking with power!

Even though I've been an adult for a while, I still struggle with confidence problems. During moments in meetings, or classes at church, or at work when there is discussion related topics, I can be in a discussion with someone or in a group setting and someone challenges my interpretation or corrects me I instantly become insecure, although they may just be helping me to articulate my thoughts. This reaction that I have can be referred to as "generational conditioning";

in simple terms, it has to do with the psychological atmosphere of my family unit during my childhood.

I think that we need to ask God for confidence. When a person or child is overwhelmed with a negative atmosphere and surroundings with little to no positive attributes to guide them, they may be exposed to this for a long period of time, if so, they may begin to exhibit those negative character traits. These people can work their whole life to eradicate these traits but occasionally they will have shortcomings. You cannot be in this state of mind if you are serious about honing in on God's will and plan for your life in your specific space and time you cannot give up. Ask, seek, knock, Jesus said, "He who asks receives; he who seeks finds, and he who knocks the door will be opened" (Matthew 7:7–8).

I think to begin to understand our destiny and purpose, our unique design; we need to first and foremost cultivate our relationship with our God and Savior and Spirit. We need to become searchers of his character, we should run after spiritual things and once we have a grip on them we need to hold onto them. We should become spiritual beings, put off carnal traits; we can do it with some daily practice. We can accomplish this with the help of the Holy Spirit, and studying and meditating on God's word daily and consistent prayer. We also should practice fasting from time to time.

Hebrews 12:14 says, "Make every effort to live in peace with all men and to be holy; without holiness no one will see God." Be a vessel of holiness. Draw close to the Lord and he will draw close to you. Replace the desires of the world which are never satisfied, with the gifts of the spirit. You will see more and sense more of who God truly is his perfect being and character. Even genuine Christians can be ignorant when it comes to really truly knowing who God is. I confess that I battle every day to pull away from the world. I want to step into the newness of life, which is found in communion with the spirt of the living God. Even other Christians can hinder our progress; they may very well have good intentions but some are very carnal and accept it as a normal function of this life.

So for God to accomplish his good and perfect will does he use the sinful nature to do this? Yes, he does; theoretically speaking, God uses sinful man in his fallen nature to bring to pass a lot of parts to his plan. God has other vehicles at his discloser to use also. God uses sinful men not because he has to, but because he chooses to. We should consider it a privilege to be partnered with the Lord in his plan. Abraham Lincoln was once quoted saying, "The good Lord must truly love people because he sure made a lot of them."

I'm still focusing on each person's design, how similar are we how different are we and what special skills, talents, gifts do we share. God uses many different design features in the animal kingdom and in the entire natural world. What will determine our uniqueness? What separates us from the other souls of humanity? Maybe it is certain levels of confidence, we know that God gives different measures of faith to each person so it is very likely that he does this with other traits, gifts, and talents, and skills. Can we really ascertain the full truth? We can continue to search, and yes, we should continue to turn over every rock and stone to confirm our true whole being that was put together uniquely to serve and glorify God and bring him great pleasure. Don't stop searching, keep running the race marked out for you uniquely, quietly, loudly, smoothly, rocky, or lovely whatever way or road you go down, but never give up.

Will we know that we have found our place? When we arrive will we have divine knowledge to confirm that we are there? God may have many roads for us to travel on. We may be in his perfect will many times over and not realize it, but staying focused on knowing him intimately is the real issue. When we rely on our own wisdom we more often than not move ourselves away from communion with the spirit. We need to be praying and practice good biblical wisdom to guide us, this is the key, and in this we can avoid needless stress and confusion.

When I observe other people and see how unique some of them are, I find it difficult to find anything special about myself. What attributes set me apart from everyone else? I feel that this is very important to understand. I know that God will use me through the whole course of my life, I may not be perfectly suited for each task but as I complete each one I will have acquired more skills and experience to bring with me to the next assignment. As I continue serving the Lord, I may confront projects that are not particularly fun or enjoyable, but this is where perseverance and long suffering will be put into practice. I personally don't expect God to reveal to me why I am one of a kind; I've searched for many years and not found it. God has his own time schedule and I am a mere man. He owes me nothing, no explanation. It's very hard to learn contentment with this situation Job was very familiar with this problem.

The place I grew up, the place I was raised, my family unit, and the atmosphere when I was a child has a role in the person God planned for me to be. It shaped my mind and my character like clay in the hands of a potter. I am still unsure about being gifted, what if I'm cursed instead could that be possible? The Devil can confuse us into believing many lies. He anoints condemnation on us like it is a blessing.

How did I become who I am? What tools did God use to mold me? When I was a child I never dreamed that my destiny was in someone else's hand let alone a divine being. The moment a child is old enough to understand some things, we train them to listen to their heart and follow their dreams. And then when they are older and able to think and reason with their mind we encourage them to set goals. And then we tell them to determine what it is they love and have some sort of passion for then, spend all your energy, time, resources, studying and training to accomplish those goals. Not necessarily the best advice, and most often they never ask the question, what has God created me for? We tend to live most of our lives within God's permissive will then we wonder why we feel unfulfilled with our circumstances. I was driving through parts of my old childhood neighborhood some time ago, and I couldn't stop myself from reminiscing and actually thinking the same thoughts that I had during those years. Thoughts of doubts about my future, my dreams, my hopes for my future, my struggles that I needed to overcome. It was as if I went back in time just for a moment it was so real. The feelings were exactly what I remembered. My mind took me back to the same dreams the same wants desires, ambitions, and hopes. But then I woke up. Those things are not who I am today, not the things I work and strive for at all. The spirit has changed my whole outlook on what is important in this life, in my life, my family's life and what God want's for my life.

In my opinion, to encourage children to make goals and plans, without one mention of God in those plans, is a tragedy.

Did you know that no two snowflakes are the same or completely alike. But all come from the same source. And God in all his creative endeavors chose to never create any two humans exactly alike. Even identical twins are not completely identical; only their outward physical attributes are similar. They can speak with the same dialect, have the same laugh, but have completely different personalities and taste. Just like snowflakes we are one of a kind. So it is with our gifts as well, Paul writes in 1 Corinthians that "there are different kinds of gifts but the same spirit who distributes them." "There are different kinds of service but the same Lord." "There are different kinds of work but in all of them and in everyone it is the same God at work." Paul here is talking about the church body of course. We need to walk with God with power and strength and to do what we need to, to be committed to find that path. Therefore, gifts are not a reflection of the person whom it is given but of the spirit. The spirit determines the person's gifts. I believe this happens only because the spirit of God has some unique ability to know all our inner parts and being. He knows each situation from our lives past, present and future, our joys, sorrows, mistakes, and disappointments. He knows all things about you and me. Only the spirit of the Lord knows what will be. He knows just how much difficulty we can shoulder; he knows how to comfort us in times of deep sorrow. He knows how to motivate us when we are overwhelmed with a task. He inspires us to rise to the occasion when we have been awake all night worrying and praying with something on our mind he is there to comfort us.

Once I was saved and baptized, I was overjoyed with my new life. I was excited about what it truly was going to do to my future. I was expecting it to be an adventure. I was naïve.

I perceived my Heavenly Father to be an unapproachable strict disciplinarian somewhat like my stepfather and mother. Little did I know he is far from that. Soon I became discouraged, I didn't know how to approach him without being so afraid that he would condemn me or criticize my every mistake. That's really all I knew, even to this day I continue to struggle with this perception. Forty years later I find myself frustrated and impatient with this. Some of these things are coming from my self-serving character I received from my childhood home atmosphere. All of us are self-centered, self-serving, and self-righteous at times in our lives. We need to "live by the spirit" to overcome these desires. It's a lifelong process to overcome these obstacles.

Understanding the will of God in our lives is easier and simpler than we can imagine. We often assume there is a grander plan orchestrated with applause and stardom the like. I had envisioned this in my mind about my new life in Christ for many years. I searched intently time after time moment by moment day after day and becoming more and more discouraged. I am trying to articulate my experiences objectively and still be sensitive. So "X" is good if "X" equals (=) God's will. Evaluate the events in your past life then you will be able to take action for your future, for the choices that will be at hand in your future.

"How do we prove that God has ever existed from eternity? How do we prove that God has a moral character, loving, merciful, patient, holy, just and good?" I quote these words from the great theologian Jonathan Edwards. Can we prove that God has a plan for each of our lives? Can we prove that that plan is ultimately good? What about our children's lives? God knows who will go astray and he will account for that in his eternal plan won't he? Can we prove this? Will it be good or bad? Is it profitable for us to analyze these things as if they have substance? Should we be subjective? It is difficult to be objective when meditating on these issues. We can be rational, logical and practical. There are obvious clues and distinctly visual observations to make. Working from a person's memory can be very helpful. To look at oneself with a magnifying glass will be an eye opener evaluating your character traits has to be done objectively.

How does God plan for our lives or does he align his with ours? He told Hagar every detail about her life and Ismael's life before he was born the book of Genesis. Jesus says in the four gospels if we ask for something in faith we will receive that for which we asked.

Does God change his purposes and plans for our lives whenever he wants to accommodate someone's request? Does God have multiple options for each person's life? Can this be true? Can we prove this? How? Do we sometimes feel as though God's plan for our lives does not align with our goals and dreams? Yes, this is what I've been getting at in this book at least part of it. So "X"= good, if "X"= God's will. Man's highest good is the will of God.

Why would anyone exchange a few minutes of pleasure and choose their own will instead of God's will? God's will leads to God's glory and our fulfillment, a life full of love, and mercy, and caring? But our few minutes of pleasures and worldly lust come and go only for a short time. But men will do this, men in the Bible did it, our brief time here on earth in this dimension is nothing but a breath.

I always read articles when I can find them that have to do with God's will, advice that sometimes tells us that we should not be searching for his complete and perfect will for our lives. Advice that says we shouldn't ponder the question but live moment to moment. That sounds great maybe for some, if you can do that. I can't. I'm a planner, lots of people are planners. I can't handle surprises, not at home or at work or planning vacations any activity that comes along it takes planning. I have a schedule of everything that needs to be done at work, task so to speak and they need to be accomplished in a routine fashion that is how I live my life as well. I set goals for everything, but I do leave room for some surprises that might surface at random. I do set time aside for that at the end of the day. You can't live life on a whim always or you will be too unorganized, God is a God not of chaos but of order.

What about times when God seems distant? Is there a possibility that during the moments of quietness when he seems as though he has forgotten about us and our existence, God may be hinting to us that we have enough on our plate at this place in our life. He might be saying be content, exhibit longsuffering right now child of mine.

God has showed his inner being to a lot of people. He has made himself visible to many of the heroes of the Bible and the Old Testament. He has revealed the destiny of many of the heroes of the Bible and told them their purposes with complete directness. Abraham was told that he would be the father of many nations. Noah was told that he would build an ark that would carry all his family and animals that God would use to repopulate the earth after the great flood. Moses was told He would go to Egypt and deliver the Israelites from their burden of slavery under Pharaoh's hand. Samson was destined to be a Nazirite. Saul was anointed the first king of Israel by the Prophet Samuel. David was chosen to be a mighty warrior and king of Israel. Solomon was told he would be given great wisdom and wealth. They were given their purposes from the start of their lives' from God. Mary and Joseph both where told who they were and what great purpose they would have a part in. These are just a few examples of scripture that show God does and can give us complete knowledge of our created purposes. So God does give foreknowledge to some people regarding their uniqueness and destiny. There are many more examples in scripture. Job on the other hand did not have this luxury. He petitioned the Lord many times for answers to no avail. He prayed over and over to God. He worshiped God in Succoth and ashes and in the end God gave him no answers, no explanations, no knowledge to the reasons for his misery, and what about the loss of his children and servants? Certainly Job suffered with sadness for the rest of his life over the loss of his firstborn children. And if he knew about the deal that was made between the Lord and Satan concerning his suffering do you suppose that might change his feelings? You can't replace the old children with new ones. But Job never cursed God. He persevered, he said "the Lord gives and the Lord takes away praise the Lord." "Blessed be the name of the Lord." "Naked I came from the womb and naked I will return to the earth" (Job 1:21).

If we only praise God for his faithfulness when we see that things in our lives' are going great and we are prosperous and happy, we misunderstand who God is and we do not fully comprehend the greatness of his omnipotence. The faithfulness of God gives us confidence and dispels worry, many examples in scripture declare God's faithfulness, this should erase worry, promote praise, we should surround ourselves with it and be encouraged. We see these truths in the story and life of Job. Through complete destruction and humiliation Job sought the faithfulness of God. His friends made an ill-fated attempt to help him; giving him advice even though their wisdom was carnal they had good intentions. But they angered God. In the end Job went before the Lord to pray for forgiveness for them. Job poured his heart out before the Lord. Job knew that the Lord would give him an answer he knew that God would be faithful; he understood the faithfulness of God.

In all of this misery Job did not sin, unwavering belief and trust in the faithfulness of God. When I don't get answers to my prayers or to God's purposes in my life, or visions of my unique gift or gifts I begin to feel rejected. No one wants to be rejected. There is no explanation that can sooth the pain and hurt from the feeling of rejection. God felt rejection, when Satan and one third of the angels left heaven. They told him we don't need you or your love, and God still feels that same emotion every day when humans choose to do what Satan and the angels chose, rejection.

God owes mankind nothing; he is not obligated to guarantee anything to sinful fallen man. We have formulated this concept.

We are constantly searching for happiness and satisfaction and validation in everything we do. We are told that God is a loving God and he wants his children to be happy. We are told that he wants nothing more than for us to enjoy our lives here on earth. This can't be further from the truth. We were created for his good pleasure not ours and until we decide to put all our energy and being into bringing about pleasure for him we will never find fulfillment. We will find our greatest contentment, pleasure, happiness, and joy not from participation in fleshly gifts or worldly passions and treasures but by enjoying our fellowship with the Lord just being in his presence. King David was a man after God's own heart. I admire David as he knew the living God in a very deep and personal way. Just reading the Psalms gives me goosebumps, I pray that I could know the Lord in that same way.

God's providence, his sovereignty, his omniscience all these attributes can be difficult to comprehend, a daunting task to say the least. I myself sometimes find it confusing trying to unravel these supernatural character traits. I will start with providence; one word that comes to mind is "foreordained" things that God has predetermined. These are things that will come to pass no matter what. I reminisce about the actions in my life that have taken place or things that I have done or not done, regrets, roads not taken, mistakes, blunders, failures. I struggle to accept this attribute of God and his providential happenings but it is a wonderful mystery to say the least. To understand this we must understand God's character, His loving, caring, patient spirit, and his complete perfect plan for mankind. He knows our circumstances all too well, the sin that recs havoc in all of creation. He has already taken that into account because he is "omniscience." Can God be omniscience but have limited knowledge? He leaves free will to humans; people make their own choices. Does God know in advance what choices they will make, or will he work within the realm of these choices? Some choices are obvious, if a person chooses to live a reckless life from that life they will receive chaos, the law of sin is constant, "what you sow you will reap," but what about God's permissive will? Can a person live within this state of relationship with their God and never ever know or realize that he has something much greater planned for their life than what they are living at the present moment? I have worked a lot of different occupations in my life. I liked some of them and I hated some. I didn't finish college mostly because of money that I didn't have. I would not apply for financial aid (loans and grants). I couldn't bring myself to borrow money for something intangible as an education. But the jobs that I did do with a certain amount of love and enjoyment still did not bring me contentment and they were still less than blue collar. I didn't love them enough to do them the rest of my life or till I die. And what can we say about God's sovereignty? He has the supreme authority and right to do as he pleases, everything is under his control.

So let's talk about joy and happiness, if we are experiencing them in our occupations are they indicators that we have found our calling and true purpose? Do these feelings or emotions validate our decision to stay or not to stay at our current job? Does finding true enjoyment in our occupation always mean that we are where we are supposed to be? What if we switch it around and say that we do not find satisfaction in our occupation, that we do not get joy and happiness from our vocation or fulfillment, should we take this to mean we are not where God wants us to be? What if our true purpose or unique gift doesn't bring us joy and fulfillment, but in fact it is our calling and our purpose for which God designed us for all along? We would probably rationalize that surely this is not right, God's plan for my life is to be happy and fulfilled, right? Does God want us to know exactly what he created us for, what he designed us for, or are we destined to stumble through life not knowing for sure his complete perfect unique purpose or plan for our life journey. I want to know what my uniqueness is. So would it be ludicrous to not tell someone; say your servant, or your employee, or your student, whatever the application may be, but all in all, you would want them to know your expectations for that individual in the arena that exists for them. You would not want them to be in the dark or clueless. You would make available to them all the necessary resources and tools that could help them thrive. You would not let each one stumble around wasting precious time and energy searching for a sign or signal from the spirit or from someone, or a close friend or a spiritual leader someone or something to validate some sort of skill or talent, or gift.

And should we feel a sense of confirmation from our emotions, joy, happiness, excitement? Or will we feel sad, or hurt, or down cast because we were hoping for something different? Will it be confirmed by our emotions? To him who much is given from him much is expected (Luke 12:48). Let's go back to discussing how we feel during the times that we are doing service for the Lord. I know that I'm in his will, but I still have this sense that he has something more profound for me to accomplish. Something that is according to his perfect will—a special purpose, so to speak. I once heard a professor declare that if you haven't discovered your unique gift you may not have one, and so you may not be a child of God. That statement hurt me to the core of my being. I could not sleep for weeks, struggling with that concept, could it be true, the theology of this principle is complicated. I will discuss this more in a few moments so try to meditate on this for a while.

These are all valid important questions I think are worthy of debate and discussion.

Purpose, meaning, fulfillment, and value are philosophical thought which requires extreme effort.

A little theology here would suffice, "progressive discloser" this is a principle that God uses. He uses it in everything in my opinion. The scriptures are full of examples, which hold true to his purposes. This is something of another curious mystery again we have difficulty explaining. It is well put in simple terms like spoon feeding a young child. The end result or the goal is to get nutrition into the growing body of the child. The parent knows that the food the child needs they may not like, so one spoonful at most, maybe less than a spoonful at a time with persistence is sufficient. But if the child spits it out, as all young children do, the parent is ready to recover the food from their bottom lip with the spoon and shove it back into their mouth hoping that in the end some or all will be swallowed by your child. This ethic has encouraged me often in my life and gave me insight in how God works to reveal his purposes.

It is a monumental task to ponder these things, to think deeply and examine life philosophically; it takes great thought and discernment. We need to put aside the distractions that clutter our minds. To search out the important and meaningful way that the Lord has in store for those who love him. True significance, I know this principle is not popular nor what we want to hear. Job may not have put much thought into his true significance. We often are unsatisfied with the results and impatient, we want answers to our questions now not later, but this principle may take a lifetime to discover, however, it will teach us patience and long suffering and protect us from being overwhelmed with anxiety as we journey to its discovery.

So I will close this chapter no closer to any answers than when I began. I've touched on many elements I believe Job may have encountered or analyzed hoping to understand more about his dilemma. I've shared my thoughts about some other characters in the scripture, those who had encounters with Jehovah just as Job did. Nevertheless, I'm no closer to any real answer or sum to the equation, so in conclusion I can ascertain, "God is God", give him the glory he deserves and question him humbly. Receive his decrees and praise him and worship him with the example Job gave us.

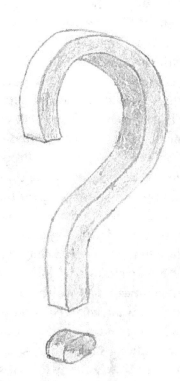

UNCERTAINTY

If we continue to serve our whole life in the capacity that we are given, not knowing just perceiving, not searching for true knowledge of our uniqueness, would we be like a common household object that Apostle Paul spoke of in the book of Romans chapter 9? The story of the potter and the clay, does not the potter have the right to make out of the same lump of clay some objects for noble or honorable purposes and some for common uses? Paul makes it clear; the will of the potter is paramount. He speaks of absolute destiny for each object designed purposely with intent in mind, specific vocation. The famous television Evangelist Joel Osteen prides himself on this motto, "Find your destiny."

I would like to share two stories of real people I knew and what happened to each of them. I would put the lives of these people in the category titled "Uncertain Purpose or Destiny." The first woman was forty-eight years old, married for twenty years, had two girls in high school, she died of a heart attack unexpectedly. She never lived long enough to see her girls graduate from high school let alone college. She would never see her girls get married or hold her grandchildren in her arms. I feel this is so sad and cruel. The second person I would like to talk about is my first girlfriend from high school. She was 16 years old when she died in an automobile accident my senior year of high school. She was the only girl in her family. She had four brothers. I still wonder why God allowed her the only girl in their family to be taken away. I don't think either one of these persons were saved or knew the Lord, this is what disturbs me. One cannot help but question the will of the Father after reading what Jesus said about the worth of sparrows and humans in Matthew 10:29, 30, 31. "Are not two sparrows sold for a penny? Yet not one of them will fall to the ground apart from the Fathers will? But the very hairs of your head are all numbered, therefore do not fear; you are of more value than many sparrows." I would conclude these are mysteries that God keeps to himself. I have also determined digging around, looking for concrete answers to God's perfect will or permissive will, will drive a person crazy, these are the "hidden things of God." I admit, I wrestle with these issues often, constantly probing for answers, even though I know is a waste of time.

STONES AND RAIL CARS

Can a man be the same as a stone? Can he be kicked and rolled around wherever to random places without any choice in the matter, with no power to change his destination? I can't help but be somewhat resentful at times for my lot in life. We have no decision making power when it comes to our existence and place in time and space. I know that living in a sin cursed world plays a major role in life, but I more often than not find it difficult to see a positive outcome going forth from my life journey with all its shortcomings and losses. I must ask, is this normal? Is there something disturbing about my inner being? Is it just sin, the fallen nature still alive and well? Is my entire life God's sovereign plan? I continue to ask these questions to give you an understanding of how I wrestle day to day with these concepts, I know many people do. If a person is striving to know God and his will for their life, they should not be content to roll around and be kicked from place to place like a stone. Also, there have been times in my life when I've felt as if I'm being pulled along a track like a rail car, not knowing where I'm going or when it will stop, in procession with other individuals to an unknown destination, comfortable, and secure not being alone, yet at the same time fearful the train will stop, then I will see where I begin the end. Having the ability or strength to rise above these fears is crucial.

It is only attainable with the help of God and his Son and Spirit. He is the one who can cover us with his love and assurance that will bring about peace to us on our journey. Jesus gave us hints about what the kingdom of God is like. We can apply these teachings to our lives today and experience them if we are willing.

Do not be anxious about anything. (Philippians 4:4)

THE OLD CLOCK
IS A THIEF

We do not have a complete understanding of time and space, it is difficult to grasp. The fact that God just exists, and eternity will be here, always here no beginning and no end, is unfathomable. Part of the problem is that as humans we only know our existence as linear. We cannot grasp this concept no matter how we try; men have wrestled with this for millennia. We also know that our state of sinfulness with the law of decay blurs our ability to see clearly. The ancient Greeks thought of time in two ways or concepts "chronos and kairos." From *chronos*, we get words like "chronometer, chronology," *chronos* is clock time; seconds, minutes, days, weeks, months, years, decades, centuries, and past, present, and future. Kairos is time as substance or matter, it is indivisible and nonsequential, kairos is God's time, and chronos is man's time. Chronos is always moving forward but kairos time doesn't move.

We can also say that chronos time is like a river always flowing, or water flowing through a pipe. You are always moving forward never going back. Kairos on the other hand is like a great ocean or lake which is immense. Our Christian view of time here on earth is like chronos, time in a pipe or river, once we reach the end and this life is done then, we will be in the unfathomable "eternal kairos," "God's time." We will still be who we were, our individual person will not change, and we will just be. So what I'm trying to do here is get to a specific point of clarity. We are here in chronos and God is there in kairos.

So to be able to, or should I say to begin to understand how to see things according to God's perspective we need to switch from chronos to kairos time, that being said, we have an invitation from God to enter into the throne room. We should not barge in and herald him as if he was our personal servant, shooting request at him like bullets from a gun. God does want a close relationship with us, remember what it feels like when you are in the presence of a close friend, who you haven't spoken to in a while, once you're finished exchanging all your thoughts and your conversation is all but wrapped up, then there is silence, then it should feel so pleasurable just being together, in each other's presence, prayer should be this way.

So let's return to the question about destiny and unique gifts or talents or purposes. God may not give us an answer for years, maybe for a life time, most of us at least the majority of Americans have a vision of leaving a legacy of something to be remembered for. I think we all dread the thought of our own story fading away or ending with no significant contribution to anything, anything that would create a positive impact in someone's life. We want desperately to be remembered; maybe this is why we pursue this uniqueness relentlessly.

If the destiny of each person is predetermined, if God knows the heart of each person before they are conceived in the womb, from the ones that chose destruction, to the ones that chose life in Christ, then why does he let them be born when he already knows their choice? He permits them to have just a short life here on earth and then condemn them for eternity? Would it not be better to just not let them be born? Many people will be born that will be lost or damned to eternal death. "Enter through the narrow gate, for the road to destruction is broad and wide and many find it, but small is the gate and narrow the road that leads to life and few will find it" (Matthew 7:13–14).

The intentions of God will never be fully understood when it comes to the destiny of human beings, God's providence, or God's perfect complete will. Men that are doomed or men that are chosen, this is a hard doctrine to accept. The clay need not and should not question the potter, many would say that this is not the kind of God that they would worship or serve. God knows who they are, they have a choice, and they have free will stained by sin. Their hearts are not pliable or soft. They cannot see; they cannot hear. God knows all these facts, they will not respond to the spirits calling.

How do we best use the time we've been given? How do we make our lives fruitful, productive, and what we do for God impact the world around us? Oftentimes I don't even pray to the Lord about certain issues because I've already made the decision, or came to the conclusion that it won't matter; he will not give me an answer anyhow, mostly because I feel unimportant and insignificant in his eyes. I developed this state of mind during my childhood. I have a store house of experiences to draw from, so a person begins to think, why bother.

Why is it so hard for some people to put their trust in the Lord? Why can't some people rise above their depression, their anxiety, their fears, their feelings of hopelessness? Some people are deeply hurting souls that can't find the path that draws them close to God. They need answers, and they need instructions on how to overcome their demons that torment them constantly.

The peace of God is not easy to find, it takes time (Chronos), a lot of time, it takes focus, it takes prayer, it takes training your mind, and it is a constant battle to continue concentrating every minute to find that peace. Staying in God's word is key for blocking out all the distractions that the world has to offer, like putting candy in front of a little child, Satan is the master of distractions, before you know it your entire life (Chronos Time) has passed before your eyes and you realize it was all about meaningless things. "Whoever loves money never has money enough; whoever loves wealth is never satisfied with his income. This too is meaningless. As goods increase so do those who consume them. And what benefit are they to the owner except to feast his eyes on them?" (Ecclesiastes 5:10–11).

So what is there to learn from all these obstacles, in the end, time, "Chronos" time controls everything I've mentioned in this chapter. Or does it? Take back what is yours, let not the clock steal from your existence here on earth in Chronos but endeavor to be in Kairos.

LILLY

Today was a sad day for our family. We had to put our little dog to sleep. Her name was Lilly, and she was a registered sable miniature Sheltie. She would have been thirteen years old in two weeks. You can learn a lot from dogs. The breeder who we bought her from told us not to put Lilly around farm animals because she will try to herd them since that's her breed, then we would have difficulty training her. Sure enough our neighbor put horses and cattle behind our property and I don't need to tell you what happened next. Lilly knew exactly what she was created for. She knew her purpose; she realized her uniqueness. And the intriguing part of this was she didn't hesitate, not once. She went right to work doing what she had never done before but knew precisely how to get the job done. She wanted to do nothing else but herd cattle and horses every time we let her outside. Now I know she is just a dog and driven mostly by instinct, but the Lord put that in her, sometimes I wish it was that easy for humans. One other little tidbit about dogs that I want to mention is their loyalty. Please don't try this but, you can lock your dog in the trunk of your car for whatever length of time, and when you open it to retrieve your pet, they are just as happy to see you as they were when you put them in there.

Just for the record, I have never tried this, it would be mean, and yes it is a great example of the loyalty and love of dogs. I didn't realize at that moment we got this little puppy thirteen years ago that I would lament over her passing this way. She was special. We mourn over them, I think in a way that our God mourns over the death of his saints. "Precious in the sight of the Lord is the death of his children." We don't create our pets we have no power to, we have no specific road marked out for them, as God has for us, similar but different, but it breaks our hearts when they pass, just like it breaks God's heart when we die. We feel helpless, from our loss and pain, emotional pain, but unlike God we are helpless, we can do nothing to soothe the hurt, wait it out and give it time, then it gets dimmer and dimmer and we heal.

We fear the things that we don't understand; they control our emotions. We do our best to hide from these elements; we loathe being free from these beasts, though they search us out to devour our being. They are experts at discovering where we may be hiding. The fear of death or the fear of non-existence, the thought of the end of our lives is frightening no matter who you are. When we watch a loved one take their last gasp of air we cringe, we are more uncertain about our destiny at this moment than any other time in our life. We are unsure what will come in the next moment of chronos. Even though we know what the promises of God tell us we still let fear be our guide. We live with death; we accept it as normal, part of the cycle of life. But the truth is it is not normal, God did not create us to die, or to accept it as normal. Why do you suppose it hurts so much when a loved one passes away, because we are not capable of enduring it. "Though I walk through the valley of the shadow of death I will fear no evil for you are with me" (Psalms 23:4).

C. S. Lewis, in one of his writings alludes to the possibility that God, in the beginning during creation may have created the animals with the gift or ability to speak and converse with other animals as well as Adam and Eve. I mean after all, the serpent did speak and converse with Eve at the tree of the knowledge of good and evil and the donkey spoke to Balaam. Then when sin entered into the picture it all changed, the earth and all its creation was cursed. Then the animals could no longer speak or communicate with one another or Adam or Eve. And God also put the fear of man in all of the animals so they would run from man if he approached them. I hope and pray that when I get to glory, when everything is new, I will not only be reunited with my saved loved ones but also I will be in the presence of my beloved pets who have went on before me. I hope they can speak and we can talk about our lives. I will be able to tell them how much I've missed them, and how much I love them, and they cannot measure the joy that fills my heart now that I'm together with them forever. I believe God will show all of those emotions toward his children when they enter his presence one day. He will be overjoyed to welcome us home, there will be grand celebrations unending. I believe that God will make everything new; he says so in scripture, according to my observation that includes all animals he created. They were innocent except the serpent, "collateral damage," so to speak. We can ascertain from the book of Genesis how much God enjoys animals; after all he created untold numbers of them to inhabit the earth. He gave life to thousands of creatures. He is a God of love and mercy to all his creation.

BIRTH   DEATH

|=========+=============+============|=====================--------------|

BEGINNING   ENDING

START   FINISH

YOUR LIFE

This is your life, are you who you want to be? Are you everything you dreamed you would be? Are you fulfilled, does it satisfy, how much do you need? Need to be content, is it all you imagined? Great questions, these are "lyrics" from a Christian song I listen to. We often think we know what we need or want but the truth is we are never satisfied or content, neither with what tangible objects we have attained or who we've become. We are disturbed and led astray, in my opinion mostly from our permissive environment and secular standards. Satan takes full advantage of this situation once again. We need help, help from a super hero; his name is Jesus. He continually preached about the kingdom of God, he gave hints I think to here and now, the present. We can live in it right here right now if we put his nature and his attributes to work in our lives. Live in the light of Jesus's presence and your light will shine brightly into the whole world. "But seek first his kingdom and his righteousness, and all these things will be given to you as well" (Matthew 6:33).

King Solomon almost drove himself mad later in his life when he strayed from God or fell out of fellowship with him. He found himself lost without purpose far from God's will. We do the same over and over again; the same temptations pull at us today, the same lust of the heart. Solomon put intense effort into finding wisdom in all his ventures. He wandered from the Lord, mostly because he became less committed to his relationship with God, and more enticed into his own matters. His wisdom came from God and I think God took some from him in his later years. I'm certain that Solomon knew his relationship with the Lord had been severed by his actions. We can learn lessons from this great story.

My hope is that somehow I can interpret what is most import-ant to all who are willing and able to make the journey. To the place where God and his inmost being can be found and understood, in the hope of discovering their true identity and perfect unique gifted-ness. This I'm certain is given to them from their creator being, out of love with grace and mercy. As I've exclaimed over and over this is not a sprint but more of a marathon that will take a life time of commit-ment. Regardless of the definition we hold of God or what we may imagine him to be, we may have convinced ourselves that we know and understand him completely and deeply into his inner workings; let's not reach the point where we become complacent in our quest to see him as he should be seen. And let us not stop searching for our perfect assignment given to us from him. William Cary once wrote, "I'm not afraid of failure, I'm afraid of succeeding at those things that don't matter, which have no eternal significance." And Dietrich Bonhoeffer once stated, "Those who truly believe are obedient, and those who are obedient truly believe." Jesus said, "If you love me, you will obey me." How much plainer and simpler could this statement be; let's find our destiny!

I decided to write this book because I wanted to help people, mostly the children of God, but also those who are lost, lost chil-dren of God, anyone who is searching for the reason for their exis-tence, and to give them comfort to know that they're not alone in the struggles of life, the dark corners of the night that haunt their souls, when it seems that God is not there. What do we do when God is quiet, when it seems as though he is nonexistent? When we long to be cuddled like a parent cuddles their little child in their arms grasped tightly never letting go. We crave for someone to whisper to us "everything is going to be just fine," "I love you and nothing will ever harm you," "You are mine and I will take care of you forever." I long for this assurance every hour of my life every day and I know other people do as well.

Come to me all who are weary and burdened and I will give you rest. (Matthew 11:28)

STAY PUT

We are sitting at the airport waiting for our plane to arrive, our flight is postponed, the plane had to land somewhere else three hundred miles away because visibility was too poor to land at our airport from blizzard conditions. We were supposed to depart two hours ago. We are tested sometimes. How do we know that we are where God has put us? We have no choice but to be patient. We could be a tree planted in a field, a seedling that grew into a giant Douglas Fir, and someone asked you how do you know God wants you to stay where you are? Your reply is, because he has put me here. But you have never seen him. No, but he sees me and takes great pleasure in my purpose here in this spot. Would you not want to go and be somewhere else, maybe nearer your God? Absolutely not! Only if he gives me a command to uproot myself, or if he comes to me. Are you content with your circumstances right now? "Yes, for I am exactly where my God and savior wants me to be" (Frances De Sales). I've been in these situations frequently and the word that comes to mind is stay. God is quiet more often than audible. We continually look for greater more grandeur purposes to kindle our egos but the truth is we flatter ourselves. My wife and I are currently sitting in the airport waiting for our plane to arrive; this fans the flames of impatience. I struggle immensely to be patient. I gaze back and forth looking and wondering about all these people, each one and their stories, their lives. I put my senses to work trying to see who they are as God sees them. Straining my mind to analyze their behavior and evaluate their uniqueness. It's really complicated without getting close to them. Most of the time when you're in an airport people are fairly reserved, they may have an I phone or android to keep them occupied, or have their nose stuck in a book like me, but casual conversation is mostly limited to their traveling companions. You can look and observe and sometimes listen to faint words and make out some but unless you engage someone in dialect you will never get near to them to know anything about them. We may be doing the Lords will without even realizing it. He is unsearchable and unimaginable. We are special and one of a kind, but he owes us nothing. We often take for granted the spiritual benefits that are promised to us. We are so arrogant in our view of ourselves. We feel entitled, we are convinced that we can send our prayers to him with our request, as an attachment, like an email message, with every want and need to meet our demands. Our greatest desires as Christians should be to meet the request of our Lord and savior Jesus Christ. Finding our uniqueness and purpose, for his pleasure will be complete in these actions. Somehow we need to turn off the need to fill ourselves with everything that hinders our sight, covetous desires, sensual desires, materialism; these things blur our vision so we fail to spot his good and perfect plan we would otherwise see. I remember some quotes my high school football coach would blurt out at us from time to time on the field, "self-abandonment, no compromise, hundred and ten percent effort, no-quitter, fully focused, play hard the whole game, team player, committed." To truly be committed totally to God and Jesus and the Holy Ghost, we need to deny every element of our carnal being 24-7. We can't know what God has in store for our lives when we are obsessed with the physical and tangible, some people hold a different view of this. "Can we draw close to God when we are so intimate with the world? Is it possible to possess all our heart's desires and still be in a relationship with our redeemer? Will we know, will we get a sign? Will we know we are still in his presence? Like stumbling through a forest, looking for a stream or a brook, would we hear a faint sound of water flowing to begin with? And as we get closer will it become louder and louder and draw us closer and closer until we can hear the rushing thundering crashing sounds of water pounding onto the rocks." That still small voice that whispers, the sound of the wind blowing, the spirits prompting the spirits leading, God wants his children to listen. We feel the need to occupy our time with something, good, bad or just killing time. People have to be busy, if we could find a way to practice stillness, stop, listen, quietness. God does not need to smack us on our heads to get our attention, he could but he chooses not to. How long do we have to be still and quiet, to hear the voice of God? The answer, as long as it takes, we need to find "kairos." God will speak to us when he is ready and only then, and when he is finished then prayer is done.

Let us speak miracles and encouragement to one another. God desires us to be inspirers, motivators, movers, and shakers not condemners, not pessimists. My complete goal for bringing to light all the unknown and unanswered situations that has, and will occur to me and the people I've spoken about, including the ancients of scripture is to help us to realize that we cannot solve any of these mysteries of life. God is the grand master of the game of life, he is mysterious and unsearchable, he dwells in unapproachable light. He alone knows his purposes and complete plan, no human can fathom his thoughts. In order for us to discover our way we should trust him and obey him. Put off earthly desires and stay in his word, feed on it. I want to encourage each person that reads this book to listen to the spirit, I mean really listen. Put aside everything that hinders and distracts us from real authentic communion with the Lord, "get in the throne room." It will not be easy; in fact it will be downright frustrating most of the time. But God is trustworthy, he will help you. Stay in the scriptures, that is paramount and pray, practice the spiritual disciplines, prayer, fasting, solitude, meditation, and fellowship with other believers you can, you must, you will.

I find it assuring that no matter what happens in my life, whether I choose wisely or foolishly, it's being directed by God and his sovereign plan. We may not find our niche in whatever we put our hands on though we should be a good and faithful servant, put the kingdom into practice. We are told, not encouraged, but told strait to the point in many verses in scripture to "be holy as I am holy be holy as your Heavenly Father is holy." Free grace does not equal free sin and the only way to be holy and overcome sin is to be filled and lead by the Holy Spirit, and this will come about by putting off the old nature and be conformed to the new nature, nature of Jesus Christ. Only then will we discover our true virtue and genuine person, the true person we were created to be, unlike anyone else, unique in nature. "You are my beloved and I have special plans for you." "I will never leave you or forsake you" spoken many places in scripture.

If you are afraid that you don't matter, if you are lost, Jesus says, "Come to me, my sheep know my voice and I know my sheep." I am awed and filled with gratitude once again at the intricacies of our creator God, how he can take sinful depraved human beings and make works of glory from them. He molds us and shapes us, refines us like a potter with clay, like a blacksmith with steel, and then burns off the impurities in the fire just by his will, "out of the ashes we will rise." Glory to God!

GRANDMOTHER

I want to say somethings about my grandmother; my father's mother. She came to America when she was just a little girl. She was born in 1898 or '99. I assume it was not long thereafter when her family moved here, probably within ten years of her birth. She was born in Switzerland along with my grandfather. My grandfather died before I was born. I never knew him. My grandmother was a devoted Catholic. She gave birth to ten children; my dad was number nine. I gained an immense amount of knowledge from the short time that I was around her, but it would be years later before I fully realized it all. Though she was Catholic, and I was not, that didn't hinder our relationship. Little did I know we only had a few short years to really get to know each other. My dad was divorced from my mother, and my brother and I were put with my mother and my stepfather. They didn't want my dad or any of his family to have contact with my brother and I, so from the age of four, I never saw my dad or grandmother, only until I could drive and have my own car did I begin to nurture those relationships. I was eighteen years old. I can now look back and see her real character through unbiased eyes. The time I spent with her I will cherish for the remainder of my time on this earth in this space time until we are reunited. I sometimes have feelings of sorrow and anger knowing I was robbed of so much time lost, not seeing or being in my Grandma's presence, I ache with resentment, not at the Lord but because of selfish people living sinful lives. I want to talk about her being, her attributes, her qualities, her virtues. My grandmother was deeply committed to her church. She committed herself fully and completely to the Catholic parish and its purposes. She was faithful to her churches vision. We live in a world today where we find few committed Christians to any church body, people are more accustomed to church hopping, going wherever the new "good feeling" takes them. My grandmother was one of the most holy human beings I've ever known. She often would take clothes to those in need of them, and if she had no clothes or money to buy some, she would sew, stitch, and mend some, or repair old used stuff. She also made blankets for many unfortunate souls who had to do without. She cooked meals for those who were shut-ins or widows. She even opened her home to those who needed a place to stay. She served meals to people who were hungry; she volunteered at the DePaul House which was a charitable organization under her church parish, she made sure needy people could get the things they needed to live. She brought joy to so many human beings, she changed many people's lives. She brought the Kingdom of God to earth. She imitated Jesus Christ. She became "holy as her Heavenly Father is holy." Amen. Today we have a difficult time just getting Christians to commit to one evening a week to do service. I can't wait to see my grandmother someday, in the new order of things to come, it will be a glorious reunion filled with joy and unending happiness and weeping tears of gladness and jubilee. She inspires me; she motivates me, to be all that God created me to be, with these chains of sin hanging from my being. It has taken me a good portion of my life to discover what she emulated in her life. I may never be like my grandmother, after all she did set the bar pretty high, but that's okay because God does have a special plan for my existence. My Grandmother practiced the gifts of the spirit and we should also. My Grandmother didn't get her United States citizenship until 1972. She was well up in years but she understood the importance of commitment. We can learn many things from this, commitment carries many definitions. When my grandmother was taken from this world it was swift, she suffered for only a brief moment, but when they wrote her obituary it was so large that it filled the whole page in the newspaper, her life glorified God completely.

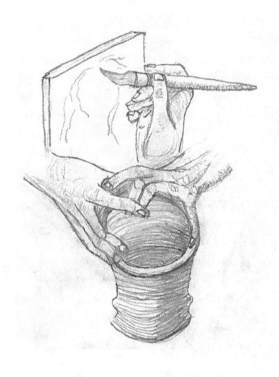

I LOVE WHAT I DO

I want to work till I die because I love what I do. I love my job, my place and occupation, what I do to make a living; it's everything I've dreamed it would be. I have the perfect vocation; they say if you love what you do you'll never work a day in your life. After all they always tell you to find what makes you happy, because you deserve to be happy while you're on this earth, I am entitled to happiness, aren't I? Isn't that our goal, to find happiness and enjoy true liberty? Doesn't God want all his creation to be bathed in true happiness and continual joy? Surely our suffering and pain with groaning's from sadness tear at his heart? If it does then that should be proof enough for him to see, for goodness sake. I will say that my observation though limited, sees our mind-set as marginal, somewhat blurred with self-centeredness. We so often shrink back to selfish wisdom. Self-righteous, self-serving, self-centered self-seeking, self-fulfillment, and self-enlightenment. I wrote in a previous chapter about some things that we are all familiar with. The most common thoughts about life from mostly secular and western wisdom, beliefs concerning our quest for joy and vocation, searching for happiness or what we think would make us happy. Sin is the cause of our inner conflict. God will give us opportunities to discover who he has planned us to be, and we have a responsibility to follow him.

"Therefore, I urge you, brothers, in view of God's mercy, to offer your bodies as living sacrifices, holy and pleasing to God, which is your spiritual worship. Do not conform any longer to the pattern of this world, but be transformed by the renewing of your mind. Then you will be able to test and approve what God's will is—his good, pleasing, and perfect will." (Romans 12:1-2).

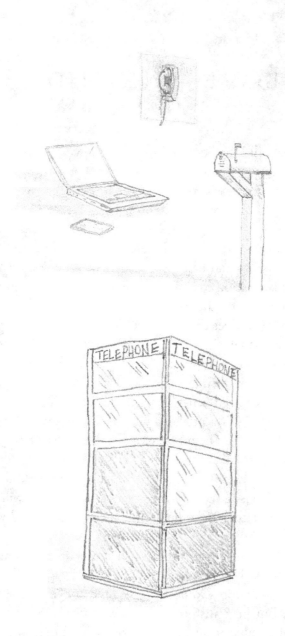

MAIL, EMAIL, TEXT

I have already shed some light earlier about my life, describing some moments of learning, disappointments, and shortcomings. I have never worked in a vocation anytime in my life where I thought, *Oh, this is it, I love this job, finally I think I've found my calling.* My point here is to help individuals comprehend this principle. You don't know what God has planned for you. Did God send you a certified letter through the postal service? Explaining his plan for your life? Or did you receive an email from him, with an attachment that has instructions typed out and on a graph, with all your appointments and everything mapped out for you year to year, with all your tasks already scheduled for you, planned by God for each year till the end of your life. How does that sound? So you just need to send him a read receipt to confirm you read and understand his instructions. Or maybe he sent you a text declaring that he has found the perfect occupation for you and he can't wait any longer to share his idea with you, but he has some questions for you to think about, and you have one week to make a decision. And last, but not least maybe he just wanted to hear your voice so he decided to call you on your android. How did he tell you? My point here is very few people know for sure what God made them for, and whether or not they were even spoken to by God. And because you think you have a love for some particular occupation, and you are convinced that that love confirms that God wants you to pursue that vocation. You see we are blinded by sin; sin separates us from God, from communing with God. So in order to truly know, we have to really be close to God, I mean, "in the throne room." You can make yourself whatever or whoever you think you are supposed be, but is it what God would create you to be? Do you presume after making yourself who you want to be, could you be transformed into who God wanted you to be all along, later in your life? Could God change you? Would you be willing? Can God be trusted, is God truthful? God will be God no matter what.

HEROES

W hen I was a little boy, I began to acquire a love for football, mostly because my friends and I loved to play sandlot football during recess at our grade school. The teachers who were on playground duty monitored our every move. We were not allowed to have any footballs during recess time or even play the game. We always found a way around the rules though. We would use any type of ball we could find to play the game. The teachers were just trying to protect us boys from getting hurt. They knew that football was a violent sport and children could get hurt playing it especially without any pads to protect them, so we were not encouraged to participate in playing football. This was the 1960s and '70s. Well that didn't detour us boys from playing the game. We would use any type of ball we could get our hands on. I knew from the moment I began to play football I wanted to be a professional football player when I grew up. My buddies and I worshiped players like Joe Namath, Fran Tarkenton, Johnny Unitas, Bart Starr, Larry Csonka, Roger Staubach. We were so innocent and naïve. My friends and I, most if not all, never had a so called "Christian upbringing," I mean we went to church most Sundays only because our mothers made us. We went to public schools, where the popular motto was you can be whatever you choose to be. I wonder if God gives any consideration to our hearts, to our dreams, or do we even have a choice in the matter of our design and talents? Does he give us a choice in the matter? What if each person had a box filled with different purposes and skills and vocations the moment they are conceived, and when they are mature enough to understand what to do they begin to reach into the box, but the kicker is they can't see what they are grabbing until they lift it completely out of the box, not knowing what they will end up with just grabbing randomly. So as they live their life they keep grabbing and picking new things from the box when they are tired or just bored with the previous choices, until one day, they finally get to the bottom of the box and low and behold they only have one thing left to pick, and this last grab is the one God had wanted them to choose all along. God being patient knew that these persons would need to experience all the so called grabs before they grabbed his perfect one otherwise they would not be satisfied and complete in the end. But would they know that this last one was the real one? Since all the other grabs had not satisfied their need for validity or did they? How do we know? If we continue to search for meaning under our own power and wisdom we end up just chasing our tail. I have knowledge of certain people who live out their whole life looking and searching but never finding. I admit I'm one of those souls. I want to be what God designed me to be, and I will continue to search, for the remainder of my existence, glorifying God as I move through chronos. If God chooses to never reveal to me everything I desire to know I'm okay with that, I will accept that. I will plug along serving in whatever capacity comes my way. So it's somewhat like playing on a game show, God is "Bob Barker" and he asks you to choose a door, what's behind door number 1? What's behind door number 2? What's behind door number 3? Go ahead and choose a door, which one will you choose? It's a crap shoot; no one knows which door to pick. Or maybe we can think of it this way, imagine that you are driving your car on the freeway that has no road signs to give you directions, you don't know exactly where you are at the moment. You observe the freeway is splitting into multiple lanes up ahead, what should you do? Which road should you take? Or should you just stay on the freeway straight ahead? Where are you going, do you know, what is the best choice? We desperately need discernment for each situation. We may not always find it, "wait on the Lord" be patient, I admit, I've picked the wrong door many times, I've driven down the wrong road many times over, I've made the wrong choice over and over. And what I have learned from these experiences is God, if he has a certain plan for you, and you go in a different direction, that door that you were supposed to choose or that road that you didn't turn on to, once you have realized that you made the wrong choice the opportunity to go back may not be possible, at least in that moment in chronos time. Regret, disappointment, feelings of failure always follow when you realize you made the wrong choice. God may be quiet for a while, letting you do it your way, teaching you and disciplining you. And the great part of this is it is most likely all part of God's perfect plan for your life. "God's providence cannot be thwarted." He is unbelievable, incomprehensible, we make mistakes, bad choices, and he weaves and meshes it into his perfect plan. God will be God. And boys will be boys.

KING DAVID

Let us look at King David and his life. I wanted to start with him mostly because my name is David, and sometimes I see parallels in my life to King David's life. But I am no king and I'm not great and I don't pretend to be great. David was the youngest male in his family. He wasn't the most masculine; scripture says he was "ruddy with a fine appearance and handsome features." David was not what Samuel expected; he assumed he would be anointing one of the eldest sons of Jesse. Scripture says, "Man looks at the outward appearance but God looks at the heart." I wonder if David was aware of his destiny. Do you suppose he was overwhelmed with questions and uncertainties? He was just anointed the next King of Israel and the present king is still on the throne hello! I'm certain he told Samuel there must be some mistake. He was a lonely shepherd boy, the youngest of his father's brood; he spent endless hours and days isolated in the wilderness, cold hungry and lonely. He fended off wild animals to protect the herd of sheep and possibly goats and other livestock. We read that David was very brave and courageous even before he killed Goliath or became King of Israel. Scripture says David rescued sheep from the mouths of lions and bears and when these wild beasts turned on him he grabbed them by their hair and struck them dead (1 Samuel 17:35–36). We know he is proficient with a sling and a stone, and it is possible that he could kill these animals with that weapon, but scripture says he struck these animals then rescued the sheep from their mouths. A bear and a lion are very quick on their feet, too fast to hit one while it is running, but if it was trying to subdue its victim that would give David sufficient time to move into range to use his sling. He had to be close because then the animals turned on him and he grabbed them by their hair and struck them dead. A full grown mountain lion and a mature black bear each have the strength of four adult men. So I can see why David was so confident to accept a challenge to fight Goliath, he would definitely be slower than the bear and the lion especially with all the armor he had on, and that to David was an advantage for him because he was accustomed to throwing stones at fast-running animals. Obviously it is still a very brave act to challenge an eight or nine foot giant man wearing armor wielding a five-foot sword and carrying a ten-foot javelin. And after he slain Goliath, David gave all the credit to the Lord. I find it difficult not to believe when David's father Jesse heard the news of his youngest son's triumph for Israel his face had to glow with pride. Once again I ask the question, did David have foreknowledge of his destiny?

1 Samuel 16:13 says when Samuel poured the oil on David's head to anoint him "the spirit of the Lord came upon David in power." But what about the time before this moment, in the wilderness, was he supposed to be a lonely shepherd boy for his entire life? We know David was gifted, he was a talented musician, he loved music, he performed for King Saul to sooth his soul after the spirit of the Lord left him and God sent an evil spirit to torment him. He was also a poet, we can read his psalms soothing and eloquent are many of them. We can see David was a deeply spiritual person even before he was anointed. But once Samuel anointed David scripture says, "Then the spirit of the Lord came upon him with power. I am overwhelmed and in agony constantly. The anxiety I deal with is exhausting, not knowing my uniqueness.

Do you suppose David experienced the same vivid thoughts and emotions and doubts, about his future or his purpose? He must have been discouraged at times in his life? I can't imagine living in that moment in chronos time, in the simplicity those people endured. They lived virtually a primitive existence. God did communicate with them though. They relied more on their faith I think, there were many foreign gods from pagan nations living in and near them from time to time so they were always tempted to abandon "YAHWEH." They lived basic natural lives committed to hard work. In comparison to our lives today, we have and enjoy luxuries beyond their wildest dreams. We have gismos and gadgets that boggle the mind. We would die in the first week if we had to live like the ancients lived. But did they question their existence, their purpose, their lot in life with all the misery and struggles they faced from season to season? How many of them do you suppose would have spent a portion if not all of their lives in deep thought, spending considerable amounts of time sorting out life, existence, purpose, design, higher powers and God's providence? I assume most of their energy was used to produce food to feed themselves and their live-stock, life was not easy for them. But they heard from God regularly, at least those who were children of the living God. When Samuel went to Jesse looking for the next King of Israel, would it have been conceivable, that he should have had foreknowledge for which son of Jesse to anoint? God waited. God wanted Samuel to begin with the eldest son then the next all the way down to the last one, which everyone there possibly were surprised beyond belief that God chose David over all his older brothers. David would fulfill God's perfect plan for eternity. Did he know? Maybe, maybe not. Did he realize he would be part of God's purpose, and be told his destiny for his own life? Possibly, possibly not, or that it included a plan for the promised messiah and savior for God's chosen children, even though David would make mistakes that would have a deep impact on his life and family and his relationship with the Lord. But God still used him with his failures and short comings to accomplish God's providence. David's most serious mistakes came when he took a break from his Kingly duties. David was lounging on his roof patio and spotted a beautiful woman, "Bathsheba."

If David chose to go to work that day he might not have sinned but, who knows we will never know for sure, but God used David's actions to further his plan universally speaking, and I'm sure David had no clue what was happening. Once again I'm enamored with our Lords providence. He has no blueprints or instruction manual, he sees our lives from beginning to end in one frame, and how he injects certain items into the precise moment in time to perfect his will is absolutely fascinating. Did David have any idea what was in store for him? We don't know for sure. I wonder what David's reaction will be when he finally sees his life beginning to end someday in glory, what will he think? Will he be overwhelmed with gratitude after he views the whole plan of God revealed partially through his own life journey? He was the least of his Fathers sons but became the greatest.

"The Lord is my shepherd I shall not want." (Psalms 23:1)

Sometime after David became king, there was a period of approximately three years in which there existed a famine. During this famine, the nation Israel had difficulty growing sufficient amounts of food. This concerned David a great deal. In 2 Samuel 21, this story unfolds. David began to seek the face of the Lord for help. I don't know what David said to the Lord; needless to say, God went straight to the point of the matter. Before we look at what God told King David, let's go way back four hundred years earlier after Moses died and Joshua became the leader of Israel.

The Gibeonites who lived near the Israelites became concerned they were in danger of being attacked by them. So they came up with a deception to convince the Israelites to make a peace treaty with them (read Joshua 9). Although the leaders of Israel were angry with the Gibeonites, Joshua convinced Israel's leaders to make a covenant with them and promised to never harm them or kill them; however, they would be indebted to the nation of Israel and become their woodcutters and water carriers for the community and for the altar of the Lord at the place the Lord would choose (Joshua 9:26–27).

So let us fast forward back to God's response to King David. God said, "The famine is on account of Saul and his blood-stained house; it is because he put the Gibeonites to death." Apparently, sometime during Saul's reign, he began a campaign to exterminate the Gibeonites. There is not much information regarding his reasoning for this action; it may very well have been political or economic; it's not completely understood. This is why the famine exists.

Now King David summoned the Gibeonite leaders to get the full truth. Sadly, the text in 2 Samuel 21 mentions nothing, or should I say, the Gibeonites mention nothing of the reason for the covenant and the deception that took place four hundred years earlier. However, they are quick to point out the evil actions of King Saul and his murderous campaign against them. Nevertheless, King

David, after hearing all the evidence, makes a decision to give them whatever they request. They say they have no right to demand silver or gold from Saul or his family or demand anyone from Israel to be put to death. King David asked, "What do you want me to do for you?" In short, the Gibeonites wanted to execute and expose seven of Saul's male descendants before the Lord at Gibeah of Saul—the Lord's chosen one (NIV). So King David said, "I will give them to you." The first two men were sons of King Saul and his wife, Rizpah. Their names were Armoni and Mephibosheth. The son of Jonathan was also named Mephibosheth; however, David had made a covenant (oath) with Jonathan, and so he spared Jonathan's sons. Also, Saul's daughter Merab had five sons. So David handed over two sons and five grandsons of Saul to the Gibeonites. We don't know the ages of these sons and grandsons of King Saul; we have little information to glean from the text.

Among other things, we don't know the character and integrity of each man or child. The grandsons may not have been of age as of yet. There are no definitive answers to many of the uncertainties that plague this story. But one thing is for sure: David knew these men or boys. He may very well have knowledge concerning the consciences of these males. And that might be what they were: adult males as the Gibeonites referred to them, but some may have just been boys. If some were just boys, then, surely, they could not participate in King Saul's campaign to exterminate the Gibeonites. However, if some were of fighting age, which we can ascertain this to be factual then, they would be loyal to their father the King and believe and trust his decisions to be true and just and accepted by God. Suppose these sons considered their father's actions to be wrong or evil, they would still be obedient to him; any rebellion to the king would be considered treason worthy of death.

Sons of Israel are required to always respect their fathers and grandfathers; they are required to be obedient. This I always thought to be true and accurate. This seems to be enough compelling evidence to prove they are entitled to some innocence. Let me demonstrate. Saul is their Father and Grandfather and their King—King of Israel. Did not his son Jonathan follow his father's lead as did these sons who were sentenced to death? If I was a betting man, I would not hesitate to wager that Jonathan had a hand in the extermination of the Gibeonites. All these males certainly followed Saul's lead. He is their dad and the king. Does this make them guilty—guilty of exhibiting allegiance? Does this leave them accountable? They were just being obedient servants. This covenant with the Gibeonites was established four hundred years earlier with Joshua, and these descendants still were angered at Saul for his actions against them. Though they failed to recollect to King David their deception with Joshua and how angry it made the Israelites, there is no proof to say any of these males had anything to do with the slaughter of the Gibeonites and little proof confirming they did. Should Saul's offspring be held accountable for his sins?

"Fathers shall not be put to death for their children's sins nor shall children be put to death for their Father's sins everyone will be put to death for their own sins" (Deuteronomy 24:16). These men or boys may very well have been convinced what their king was doing was just and right and well-deserved punishment for the Gibeonites and the lie they made to Joshua four hundred years ago. Furthermore, these sons might have been convinced their father the king was the chosen instrument of the Lord to execute the punishment unto the tribe of the Gibeonites that was long overdue. Was it possible these sons never approved of their father's quest to wipe out the Gibeonites? Perhaps similar to King David and his brood, they did not honor him or walk in his ways or follow his lead, especially when it came to truth and integrity. Nevertheless, there is no solid proof to provide us with evidence to show these men deserved to be sentenced to death. Is it possible they were doomed from birth? Could this be their purpose for being born? If so, then there was no way out for them, no alternative destiny or purpose. They had no power to change their life story.

Perplexing enough already, but could their lives have had a more positive outcome? Let's say God illustrated all the outcomes of each son's lives individually well before they were held accountable, would this be enough to change the destiny of each one? The text doesn't even give us the names of the five grandsons. I wonder why. We can very well ascertain King David knew their names; after all, he was part of the extended family since he was married to Saul's youngest daughter, Michal.

It can be very difficult for the reader to make heads or tails of this story due in part to the tragedy of these males and the sorrow it brought to each one's family. Would these sons embrace their destiny and want to complete God's will and perfect plan for their lives knowing they would be executed for the broken covenant brought on by King Saul's actions? Furthermore, was this these males special purpose or God's permissive will? And if they knew this from before their birth, I'm sure they would not want to be born. Who would? Shall the masterpiece accept the master plan set in place by the master creator or ask, "Why did you make me this way for this purpose?"

How about the response of King David? He spoke in other scripture concerning the remnant of the household of King Saul. He enquired as to if there was anyone left. He was told about Jonathan's son Mephibosheth. This tells me David may not have known Saul's other sons or grandsons, so if this is true, then he would know nothing of the chosen men's character or their age. David was still loyal to King Saul, wanting to show kindness to his household or remnant although maybe more for the sake of his love and covenant with Jonathan. Nevertheless, King David still would honor the king whom he served. David was always quick to honor and protect the king; he never harmed King Saul. He served him and played music for him. Furthermore, after King Saul's death, David spent much time during his early days as king cleaning up the messes Saul left behind. Surely, when the Gibeonites came to King David, one would suspect he knew about the covenant and deception with Joshua four hundred years earlier. One must ask why David would not enquire of the Lord once more after he spoke with the Gibeonites, possibly to avoid any more bloodshed. He knew they wanted blood; they told him so. Those who were a part of Saul's family were not responsible for his actions, and this bloodshed was about to bring sorrow and weeping for the remainder of everyone's lives who loved these men or boys or both.

This broken covenant with the Gibeonites fell on the remnant of Saul, which, in turn, was the reason for the three-year famine in the land. I ask the question: Was there no other alternative to be found? The Gibeonites wanted blood though they had the opportunity to request things of greater value. Is this justice? Why would King David not resist their demands for blood and persuade them to settle for something of real value rather than murder? These seven sons may very well be innocent. King David doesn't hesitate; he gives them these males, no questions asked. Their fate is sealed. These men and boys are hung. Whoever they are, sons or grandsons, David gave blood for blood. These children are no better off than Job's children. Both are killed to prove a point; they were born to die. The difference may be, among other things, Job made provisions for his children's sin, just in case. He made extra sacrifices to the Lord for their sins.

And the actions of King David, what anguish must have befallen him in regard to the sorrow taking place in the lives of these relatives of the sons and grandsons of King Saul. Job was familiar with the character of his children. This is the reason for his extra sacrifices, I believe, but David may not have known these son's character. Maybe he did, and if he didn't, he would always question his decision. What can we learn of God's character and will from these things that took place in the lives of these masterpieces?

Destiny, purpose, gifted, pieces of pottery kiln fired for this plan, or beautiful paintings with unique brushstrokes, we are uncertain, but one thing is certain: these souls fulfilled God's assignment. Ironically, just like Uriah, they were obedient to the king and gave their lives for an honorable act, just as they may have been obedient to King Saul, this time, obedient to King David—once more, one last time unto death, just like Uriah. Note: For those who are uncertain who Uriah was, he was the husband of Bethsheba, the woman King David committed adultery with. For a complete account of Uriah's destiny, read 2 Samuel chapter 11.

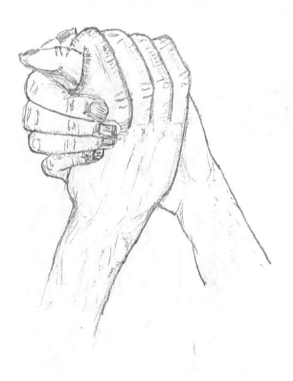

PALS

Foreordained, what exactly does this principle mean? Something which has been planned from the beginning of something? I'm compelled to return to this issue once again. When I was a teenager, I had many friends; however I only cultivated a handful of close relationships, these were my pals. I developed a special bond with each pal, individually. I did many activities with each one, and from time to time we all did some things together, like hanging out after school sports, and playing board games. We did some good things, but also, some things not so good. Teenage boys from a secular public school, one can put two and two together, and get three, not four, if you know what I mean (ha ha). Some years later, one of these pals, who was my best friend in high school, married his high school sweetheart. The two of them raised three children, and thirty-six years into their marriage he murdered her. Then he made an attempt to make it appear to be an accident. Unfortunately for him, that didn't work out to well. He now sits in prison doing a twenty-seven year prison term, he was fifty-something. One of my other two pals was also married; he was a drug and alcohol counselor.

One day, his wife let him know she wanted out of their marriage she was done. She left him and he went outside and shot himself dead, he was fifty-something. The last of the three had an alcohol and drug problem, in school I never thought too much about it we all participated, it was the thing to do, but come to find out he never grew out of it like most of us did. He couldn't leave it alone drink after drink with drugs; sad to say I got word in March of this year. He died of liver disease, what a waste, he was fifty-something. These three pals of mine wasted their lives. The fallout from each situation is enormous; each family will suffer pain and agony for the remainder of time they have left on this planet. Each of these lives are different, same destiny but different, not a good one, but a horrible one. In each life road or path someone died. Death from murder, suicide, and addiction. What are the odds, out of these three and myself, I'm the only one who has taken a different road. This is a mystery to me, why me, how is this possible, why am I more fortunate than they? They were no different than me.

What if, let's imagine for just a moment that at some point, these friends of mine had an opportunity along the way to see a glimpse of their final destiny; do you suppose this would be enough to sway them, to take a different road? What if my best friend's wife saw her future well before she married him, what if she had a dream or vision do you think she would have second thoughts about marrying him? And my friend who shot himself, he could council others, but not himself. Or my buddy with the addictions, was his DNA the villain here, could he not help himself? In each one of these lives we see tragedy. Perhaps if they had foreknowledge they would have had a better opportunity and their lives would have had a positive ending. I lament for these pals of mine so many memories, will I ever see them again, all I can do is hope and pray their endings are more hopeful in eternity than what they were here in this physical existence. "Indeed, the vary hairs of your head are numbered. Don't be afraid; you are worth more than many sparrows" (Luke 12:7).

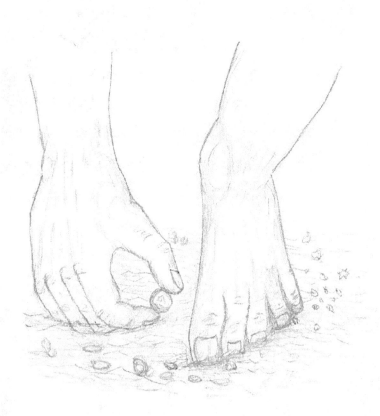

PEBBLES

I think about the odds in every situation, it's like pebbles scattered on the beach, randomly thrown there by the ocean's waves, washing them ashore, which ones are special, how do we know? Only until you pick them up and hold them to a polishing wheel will you know which ones can be used for some useful purpose, or are the most beautiful. Will some shine exquisitely, while others are just common stones? What makes certain ones desirable and others not, what's the difference?

How do we determine which ones to choose, the ones that will shine the brightest when polished? Knowing God can do all things inspires me to consider his choices when it comes to human beings. He knows beforehand who will shine, who is a common stone and who will be special. Amazing! My mind is filled with questions; it's so profound and mysterious. God prides himself in showing us humans, that we cannot predict his actions or choices. He always does exactly the opposite of man. I'm speaking of generations of people that are chosen by God to do his will. Like pebbles scattered on the beach, we are scattered through time, "chronos" and his chosen people, are randomly thrown among generations of human souls wandering aimlessly on this planet. I hope I can fulfill God's plan for my life completely, whether I am a polished beautiful stone or common pebble.

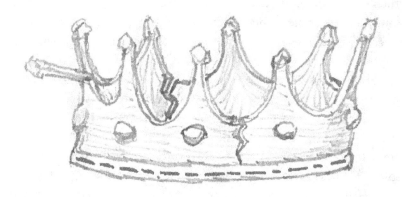

SOLOMON

Even though King David committed horrendous sins which separated him from God, he did repent, and was restored back to a full relationship with the Lord, or at least almost full. I'm not so sure if his son Solomon ever did. I have always been intrigued by the story of Solomon. He was so blessed by the Lord. He demonstrated great discernment when God spoke to him. He could have asked for anything, I don't have to elaborate as most people know the story well. This is one of the only times I know of in scripture where God almost seems to exhibit genie like qualities, like a genie in a lamp, but let's be clear, he is not a genie. We know that King Solomon, when God said, "Ask for whatever you want me to give you" (1 Kings 3:5) Solomon asked for wisdom to rule successfully over these people. So God, instead of keeping these wishes to himself and just blessing Solomon behind the scenes, went ahead and expressed his motives to Solomon. God said, "Since you asked for wisdom and not for selfish things, not for long life or the destruction of your enemies, not for great wealth or prosperity or lasting peace, now then I will give it all to you. You will be blessed beyond measure." Israel will flourish. How did this fit into God's perfect plan, His future plan? How will this affect Solomon's destiny? God blessing Solomon with unending generosity flowing like a river, how will that affect the future? What will this do for the destiny of the nation of Israel? I ask these questions to inspire some thought for the story and where it will end up. People journeyed from near and far to witness the wisdom of King Solomon. Israel enjoyed many years of peace with their neighbors and prosperity. What do we know about Solomon's attitude; did he become somewhat smug and arrogant over time? He exhibited great zeal for woman, woman of many ethnic groups who worshiped pagan gods. Why would God allow this to take place? Once again, I ask the question not to challenge God, only to gain a more complete understanding of his motives and to learn more about his character. He could have stopped what was taking place but he was quiet, why? Solomon exchanged his relationship with the Lord for sensualism. He replaced worship to the Lord for building and erecting pagan idols to pacify his many wives. Why would Solomon compromise his actions and indulge himself in worldly passions? Did he forget the first two commandments of the law? He somehow was blinded.

First Kings 11 says that in his old age, "Solomon's heart was not totally committed to the Lord as his Father David's was and Solomon went after other gods." To satisfy his many wives. How did this happen, did Solomon not witness his Father David's devotion to the Lord? He knew what would take place if he fell short. Did he simply forget, or was he complacent? Then after the Lord spoke to him regarding his sin maybe he became discouraged and thought well, it's too late now, and repenting now isn't going to change God's mind.

Solomon may have reasoned, I will have to live with the consequences of my actions. I'm not sure what was going through his mind at this point, remarkably though he seemed content with leaving the altars and idols of the pagan gods' standing. If Solomon was truly remorseful for his actions, I would have thought he would do the opposite and remove the altars from the high places. Had Solomon become proud, was he infested with self-centeredness? Was God aware that this was bound to take place; he has a full view of Solomon's complete life line or existence from conception to his death? But was this God's plan for Solomon, was this his plan for Israel? God dropped his judgment on Solomon for his sins and this will affect Israel as well. Chaos will come to the house of Solomon and Israel will be chastised and cut off. This is a harsh penalty and a serious consequence, well deserved from God's point of view. Solomon, according to scripture, spoke with God in the first person more than once.

In 1 Kings 11:9, God refers to Solomon's attitude, I assume it was a bad attitude, like scolding a little child for their disobedience, there will always be a reaction to our actions. God will forgive but, he will not take away the percussions that will develop from them. This is the heavy price of sin, God was still somewhat merciful to Solomon, he let him remain on the throne until his death. God could have ripped it from his hands immediately though he did not. I'm speculating maybe this was planned by God to be part of the punishment rendered to Solomon. To give him some time to reflect on the choices he had made up to this time in his life, the mistakes that took place from his poor decisions. What a great disappointment this must have been for him. I assume he was so overcome with guilt and shame knowing the grief that God would bring upon Israel when he was gone. I believe Solomon became somewhat confused, especially when you read the book of Ecclesiastes. I get the impression maybe he was going insane or going mad. He seems desperate to make heads or tails out of life; this may have been years after God gave him the verdict regarding his future and Israel's. I must ask the question, did God plan all of this from the beginning, how will he know the hearts of humans before they are created, how does he know their motives, or whether they will be good or evil?

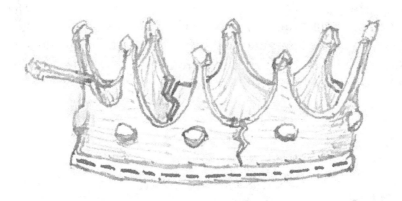

KING SAUL

The story of King Saul is one more that sparks my curiosity. Saul, being the first king of Israel could have been the greatest king, but "absolute power corrupts absolutely."

In 1 Samuel 8, Israel is demanding a king be set before them like the other nations. God replies to their request that he is their king, but Samuel returns to the Lord to explain that Israel wants a human king not a God king, "give us a king to judge us" (1 Samuel 8:6). Saul was the son of Kish a Benjamite, and a mighty man of valor (1 Samuel 9–1:2). Scripture says Saul was a choice and handsome man and that there was not a more handsome person among the sons of Israel. Saul was one head taller than any of the people. I want to investigate the events that took place in Saul's life that led to his demise and contributed to his falling out of favor with the Lord.

Hopefully, this will enable us to see some of Saul's inner secret character which God sees, and reveal a little of God's character as well. The first thing I noticed from the beginning of the text in 1 Samuel was the swiftness in which this all took place. God wasted no time getting a king for Israel. The timing was smooth with no hiccups. One day, Saul is out searching for his father's lost donkeys and he returned home king of Israel. Saul was from the least of the tribes "Benjamin" and the least of those families from that tribe and now he is the top dog so to speak. So what about Saul, what can we learn from him? Do we know why God chose Saul to be king? Saul came from the least of the tribes of Israel. God has an uncanny way of choosing, choosing from the weak, from the sick, from the least of everything and everyone to do his will and accomplish his purposes. All through scripture he picks people who are in no way desirable by human standards. Saul seems to be the devoted type, committed to doing what's good and right. I notice from the beginning he is a good son to his father and an upright person full of integrity. So what changed in him later? It's interesting to note that when they brought all the tribes together to choose a king by lot the tribe of Benjamin won, and then Saul's family won by lot from all those Benjamin families, and then Saul won by lot from the men of his family. God had planned and executed this all for his purpose. But what I find so remarkable, for when Samuel anointed Saul God changed Saul's heart. Then when Saul met the prophets who arrived at Gibeah in 1 Samuel 10:10, "the spirit of the Lord came upon Saul mightily," so he was also prophesying, so how did God change Saul's heart?

If God can change the heart of King Saul then it should be simple for him to change as many hearts as he sees fit, but he hasn't. Maybe every heart is different some are soft and pliable and some are hard, resistant even impenetrable. I should mention that this is a time well before the outpouring of the Holy Spirit or Pentecost. God only dispersed his spirit to certain people at this moment in Bible history. I also find it interesting that although God gave Israel a king he was reluctant at first and offended. He expresses his frustration to Samuel that Israel has it pretty good at the moment, and they would not be happy with a man king. If God knew beforehand that he would give them a king, why did he expel so much energy and effort to resist, trying to dissuade them? Does this say something about God's character? Isn't God omniscience, or omnipotent? Does this mean God is not all knowing and all powerful? I'm being analytical, trying to ascertain God's qualities and motives here. This seems strange to me. God even touched the hearts of the valiant men who escorted Saul to his home, but not all the men, I wonder why some and not others? And Saul put to rest any doubt that may have been lingering about his qualifications soon after he was anointed king over Israel. During the battle and following the victory over the Ammonites he proved his great worth, leadership, and courage. I marvel at his response in 1 Samuel 11:6, "Then the spirit of the Lord came upon Saul mightily when he heard these words and he became very angry" the words he heard were the threats from the Ammonite men against the people of Jabesh-Gilead. In his anger he did not sin, in his anger he was calm, in his anger he knew precisely what he was about to do, remarkable. Saul was emulating God by God's spirit, this is the conclusion I have ascertained from this story. Saul rendered wisdom to the people soon after his army struck down the Ammonites. The people asked, "Who were the ones against making Saul King, we should put them to death," Saul replied, "no one shall be put to death today, for this day the Lord has rescued Israel." That's an amazing statement given from King Saul full of wisdom and discernment. King Saul reigned over Israel between thirty and forty years depending on the translation you read there are some missing parts of the Septuagint so scholars are not sure but anyway, he probably reigned almost as long as King David reigned. I don't know what sparked King Saul's free thinking that led to his demise as king but, he freely disobeyed Samuel and God. He performed a sacrifice instead of waiting for Samuel the priest to return and perform it. He failed to carry out God's full instructions in which he was to completely destroy the Amalekites, everything, men, women and children, all livestock, including sheep, goats, horses every living thing, and to take no plunder period. Does Saul deserve forgiveness? Does he deserve mercy? King David received forgiveness and mercy from God. Why, do you suppose God decided to remove Saul as king? After all God was upset with Israel for asking for a man king, maybe this is the reason? Saul had never worshipped other gods as Israel had, yes Saul was somewhat impatient at times and stubborn, so was Moses, Peter, Jonah, Jacob, and Solomon and I could keep going, but I can't put my finger on it completely why God had given up on him.

First Samuel 15 is very sad in my opinion, Saul seems genuinely convinced he has obeyed the Lord in carrying out the instructions given him to completely destroy the Amalekites until he receives his chastisement from Samuel. He is sure he has been obedient to the Lord in his actions, but then, after a long and hard rebuke from Samuel, Saul's eyes are opened and he exclaims, "I have sinned" this to me is genuine repentance. Isn't it? Then Samuel said once again to Saul it is to late the Lord has given the kingdom to someone better than you, but Saul pleaded once more for mercy and wanting him to return with him to worship the Lord, and as he reached for Samuel he tore Samuel's robe then Samuel exclaimed, "He who is the glory of Israel does not lie or change his mind, for he is not a man that he should change his mind" (1 Samuel 15:29).

Saul says once again, "I have sinned." Has God not changed his mind ever? God has not lied but he has changed his mind at times in scripture I'm certain. I know that Saul did do some evil things in his life but, so did King David and King Solomon. Did God harden Saul's heart? Only God knows the hearts of men. Samuel loved Saul very much I don't know why, scripture says Samuel mourned for Saul and did not see Saul again for the rest of his life. In 1 Samuel 16:1, God even asked Samuel, "How long will you grieve over Saul, since I've rejected him king over Israel? As I continue reading through the story it seems as though Saul is overcome with grief and despair. He desperately seeks the Lord, pleading for the Lord to speak to him. Is this genuine repentance, he's showing signs of remorse and sadness? Samuel has since died, so Saul cannot seek him out for guidance. Why would God leave Saul in this state? If Saul would have just been patient, I'm sure the Lord would have come to him in time; Saul needed to continue to be devoted in worship and righteousness and become the honorable king he was anointed to be. In a previous chapter I posed the question, what will you do or what would you feel if God revealed to you his plan for your life from the moment you were old enough to understand and showed you your complete life beginning to end. If Saul had seen his life would he want to live it, or would he ask God for a new one? He may have been overcome with grief that the Lord had given him such a cursed life, I surely would have. He may have not wanted to even be born. Most every-one wants to be remembered for something significant. I can't help but feel empathy for Saul, he asked Samuel for mercy, he said, "I have sinned against the Lord and done a terrible thing."

King David also exclaimed to the prophet Nathan "I have sinned," but in this case God forgave David, and let him remain king. I could keep writing about Saul's life there is a lot to look at but, I keep coming up with the same conclusions, obedience, and the state of the heart. At the close of the story Saul and all his sons were destroyed by the Philistines and their bodies were desecrated, then they received a meager burial service. They were honored little in the end. In my opinion this was a very sad and tragic story, but who am I, I'm just a man who lies and changes his mind.

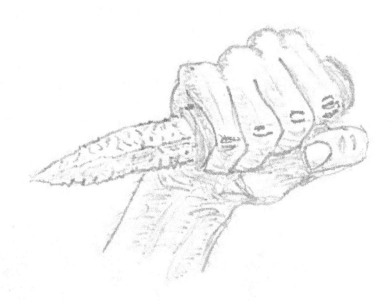

CAIN

The story of Cain is a remarkably sad one also. Cain was a man of misery. I've read and studied this story over and over trying to grasp why God became so dissatisfied with Cain and his offering and pleased with Abel's. I was unable to ascertain any difference between their offerings scripture is very vague and short. So in order to get to the bottom of this mystery I needed to dig deeper. I spent some time using other study materiel and resources from other books and interviews with pastors and teachers to further shed light on this subject. What I did find concerning those passages of scripture in question was fascinating, things I never thought of before. Some of it may be speculative and not definitive. When Adam and Eve sinned they became aware of their nakedness, so God made garments of skin "leather" to cover them, this act, was most likely the very first blood sacrifice, performed to cover them or cover their shame, the very first animal to die for human beings. Bible scholars sometimes refer to this as the first ordinance or part of the first ordinances instituted by God to Adam. They will not be recorded until Moses gives them to the Israelites in the desert of Sinai. Moses will write the Levitical laws to make things clear.

So now let's return to the story of Cain and God. We now know that the blood atonement was to be practiced in order to cover sins. So this means that an offering had to be with blood of a sacrificed animal, but Cain came without one, with no blood. He came with something else, Cain offered fruit and vegetables, grain wheat, Abel on the other hand, paid close attention to what his Father Adam most likely practiced, he more than likely told him, "You must have blood you need to sacrifice an animal." Now I'm purely speculating here because this is not in the text. So when Cain received his chastisement from the Lord, for bringing the wrong offering, God did not tell him to bring a sacrificed animal, he just said to him, "If you do what is right, then you will be accepted." Why God never reminded him of the requirement is not known, but I think that God knew all along, that Cain, knew the requirement but chose to be stubborn and bring his own offering, so he could be different than his brother Abel. What if he did know the requirement, but had no experience in how it was to be performed, he should have asked for help from his brother Abel, certainly Abel would have gladly helped his brother do the right thing. Cain would have had to humble himself and that was out of the question, you see Cain had a bad attitude of the heart, which motivated his disobedience. Cain let anger burn in his heart and bitterness subdued his mind and body. God most certainly watched this take place from the foreground, and let Abel be murdered at the hands of Cain.

I ask myself this question every time I read this story why? This is the same scenario as what took place in the Garden of Eden, God could have intervened, but he didn't, why? As a parent I pride myself in keeping my children safe from danger and poor choices, God is not exactly that sort of a parent. Sure he meets our needs and guides us in life, but he chooses to let us make some mistakes. This is purely to help us grow in wisdom, and to conform to habitual prayer. Back to my question, Cain lived a long life, God possibly let Cain live, why? To let him suffer for his actions, and God put a mark on him not just to protect him but also to remind people who he was and what he had done, but also I think it was to shame him for his horrible act. God must have known all along what was the center of Cain's heart. This story was all a part of God's perfect plan.

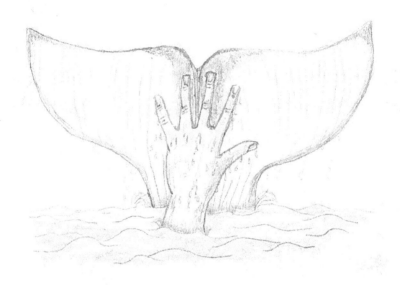

JONAH

This is about the story of Jonah. He was given specific instructions from the Lord to go and preach to the city of Nineveh. They were a wicked pagan metropolis housing approximately 120,000 people. Here again God has revealed a special purpose or plan designed for someone with a unique gift or talent that he wants them to use for his will, Designed for Jonah son of Amittai. Jonah has other plans He runs. Surely God could find someone else to do this task, Jonah wants no part of it, and so if I was God I wouldn't waste my time with Jonah. There has to be other people God could use? I see nothing special concerning Jonah, he grumbles through the complete story all the way to the end. Jonah is not one bit motivated about this plan for his life. I think this parallels our lives more often than we are aware of. Sometimes we are moved by the spirit and we hesitate to respond in faith, maybe out of fear of the unknown or there may be other obstacles that overwhelm us. There were a few reasons Jonah was resistant to God's mission for him to go and preach repentance to Nineveh. Jonah knew the people of Nineveh were pagans and not Hebrews and they worshiped pagan gods. This convinced Jonah perhaps these people were undeserving of mercy and he was not sure why God would expel so much care for them. So Jonah made the choice to disobey God and run, how foolish, he really thought he could hide from the creator of the universe, how we are like Jonah. I chuckle. The second item I want to address is Jonah's conclusion that, even if he went and witnessed to the people of Nineveh they were not going to repent and change their wicked ways, but they did. And God forgave them. And in the end Jonah was more determined to hate them and hope they would not change. Why does God explain every little detail in this story to Jonah? After all that takes place Jonah still had a bad attitude, even after he finished his task for the Lord, and why does God not chastise him more severely for his lack of concern or love for those human beings? Aren't we the same today? Let's show love even when we don't see the whole picture. Jesus replied, "Love the Lord your God with all your heart and soul and mind, this is the first and greatest commandment and the second is like it; love your neighbor as yourself" (Matthew 22:37–39).

ENOCH

This is the short account of the life of Enoch. I have much to question concerning Enoch; unfortunately, there is not much substance to his life. In my opinion, God created Enoch specifically to pave the way for Noah to be born. He is already planning to flood the earth and he has foreordained knowledge of Noah's righteousness and blamelessness, and God will give the talents and skills of building with wood to Noah to achieve this endeavor. Enoch was Noah's great-great- and great-grandfather. Enoch was also blameless and righteous it's obvious from scripture (Genesis 5:24), "Enoch walked with God and then he was no more, because God took him away." We could very well say that this scripture is talking about some kind of rapture, I'm speculating of course, but it is interesting. I like to think that Enoch was so righteous and blameless perhaps the Lord was rewarding him for his character, but I'm more apt to believe as soon as he fathered his children, preferably as soon as he fathered Methuselah his purpose was finished. Methuselah will then father Lamech who will father Noah, God's providence at work. Do you suppose these men knew their purposes, or the reasons for their existences? We know Noah walked with God and he spoke to Noah about his complete plan for humanity, but did he speak to Enoch about such things, we know Enoch walked with God. I love investigating these stories they permeate with mystery and imagination for the reader, at some point we have to just let them lie. We will let them strengthen our faith.

BE WITH US

Can your mind comprehend the knowledge of the Lord? Can you understand God's plan for your life from beginning to end? Can you fathom all there is to your existence if he revealed it to you in one moment, similar to flying a spaceship through the galaxy at the speed of light, would it not overwhelm the senses of the human body and the mind? You might want to die or the fear could be enough to kill you. God is fully aware of our weak and delicate frame. He doesn't want to load us down with burdens we can't carry; many times in scripture we have the assurance "he will be with us."

There are many stories in the Holy Scriptures illustrating these principles of human insecurities. First and foremost, we know the Spirit of God was not poured out to everyone in the Old Testament. God was discriminative when doling out his spirit. Many of the ancient prophets left everything to walk the path God marked out for them. He was present and audible with them. God spoke to them face-to-face though they could not see his face for they would die. Some of these men still had doubts from time to time. Abraham, the father of all nations was in doubt many times, Gideon, Elijah, even Moses, though these men walked side by side with God, and spoke with him they still lacked faith in moments of despair. Tell me, how many of us you or your neighbor, if God came down from his throne in heaven to speak to you face-to-face and told you he had a mission for you, and a plan for you which would require the rest of your life would you rather stay put where you are?

Maybe you would be brave enough to debate the creator of the universe, plead your case, not a wise thing to do. Sorry, God, but I have a plan for my life and what you are asking won't fit into my endeavors. I can't do that for you, Lord. You may have to give up everything about your life, how could you say no to God, your future may depend on your decision, yes or no? God revealing to you his divine plan for you and you are turning him down; he created you for this specific purpose in this specific time and space. He knows you better than you know yourself, can you trust him, can you trust yourself? He will be with you. "I have called you by name; you are mine. When you pass through the waters I will be with you; and when you pass through the rivers, they will not sweep over you. When you walk through the fire, you will not be burned; the flames will not set you a blaze "For I am the Lord your God, the holy One of Israel, your Savior" (Isaiah 43:1–3).

MOSES

In Exodus 33:12–23, I find these scripture verses so fascinating for years I've tried to fully comprehend their full meaning. Moses is speaking to God in person he has a first-hand account of God and his plan for the Hebrews. Moses is still hesitant, not sure. God is ultimately speaking to Moses revealing his plan for redemption and the fulfillment of his promise. Moses is compelled to see all of God's glory but God will not allow it, perhaps we can ascertain this is due to the sinfulness of Moses, after all he is not redeemed as of yet. "No one can look upon the face of God and live" (verse 20).

Jesus will remove this obstacle, he will be our sunglasses, he will be our filter, he will be our shield, and Jesus will protect us from the wrath of the living God. So for Moses at this time God will show him his glory but God's hand will shield Moses's view of God's face. Reading on through chapter 34, Moses still remains in doubt and fear of the Lord. When God returned the next day and Moses came with the second set of stone tablets for the Lord, Moses asks God once again, "If I have found favor in your eyes, he said then let the Lord go with us. Although this is a stiff necked people forgive our wickedness and our sin, and take us as your inheritance." I'm perplexed somewhat; this is not the first time Moses has petitioned God to go with him, God showed Moses his glory and his plan for redemption but he still has doubts. Would we still entertain these same familiar fears and insecurities if God spoke to us in person as he did with Moses? Perhaps we need to remember these were people living in the bronze and iron age of time, having seen a "being" coming to life from a burning bush must have been frightening or just appearing out of nowhere would be a supernatural event that would flesh out all yours fears and cause severe trembling and shaking. Moses most likely was comfortable living under Jethro's tent, little did he know God was about to change his world for the rest of his days on this earth. Moses was compelled to resist, he was certainly so overwhelmed with fear and questions he had no idea what to expect or what to do. What would we do if this happened to us, would we run like Jonah, or have every excuse in the book to get out of doing our purpose for the Lord? Interesting to note Moses's father in-law was a priest of Midian a descendant of Abraham's son Midian born from Abraham's second wife Keturah who he married after Sara died.

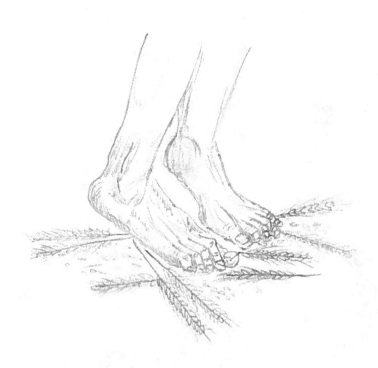

GIDEON

Gideon was from the weakest of the tribes of Israel the clan of Manasseh, the least of the families; this is the same familiar process we have seen again and again. God does this often; he chooses people from lowly ordinary places, weak, poor families with little to no honor from their tribes or villages. We have seen this same scenario in many of the stories in scripture. We can observe some of God's character from these stories. He loves an underdog; he takes the weak and makes them strong in order to show his glory. I think this is his way of saying he needs no help to prove his point in accomplishing his will. I can't understand it all, I know there is more to the reasons for his actions in everything, these truths do say a bit about his personality, his passions, and his thoughts. Is He yearning for us to see these traits? Is he purposely spoon feeding his inner being to each one of his chosen few? Once again, he gives strait forward instructions to a man from the weakest of tribes and least of the families to go and destroy the Midianites, he just spoke to Gideon face-to-face it may have been a theophany (manifestation of God) but Gideon is not convinced that this "being" is really God. Gideon wants God to give him a sign, he just spoke to God face-to-face and he still has doubts! How often do we doubt each moment of the spirits call? Perhaps we are fearful it may not be God speaking to us. Similar to Gideon's feelings, though he spoke with an audible deity, we aren't allowed that luxury, it's not at our disposal. Gideon is remembered for his fleeces, I would have thought that; when he petitioned God to do this, did his request not insult God's character, after all wasn't God's word sufficient for Gideon? God said he would go with him and he did just that. As Gideon gathers warriors for his fighting force God once again demonstrates his plan by whittling the fighting force down to around three hundred men or so. I think this is done to show Gideon that his God can do mighty and impossible feats without human strength. This should kill any doubt left in Gideon's mind. We don't necessarily see God do these remarkable things today but, I suppose the real lesson here is Gideon was shown his destiny with these tasks.

"And we rejoice in the hope of the glory of God. Not only so, but we also rejoice in our sufferings, because we know that suffering produces perseverance, perseverance, character, and character, hope. And hope does not disappoint us, because God has poured out his love into our hearts by the Holy Spirit, whom he has given to us" (Romans 5:3–5).

ABRAHAM

I have read and studied the story of Abraham many times. He was given his purpose and destiny from God when he was seventy-five and Sarah was sixty-five, but keep in mind that Abrahams father Terah lived to be 205 years old so, middle age at the time was more than likely around eighty to one hundred. Scripture says that Abraham and Sara waited for a son till they were beyond child bearing years. Years earlier when Abraham questioned God about his timing for a son explaining to God his estate would go to one of his servants (Genesis 15:2–3). God told him a son would come from his own body, so God made a covenant with Abram telling him his descendants would be as numerous as the stars in heaven and the land he was going to would someday be his. Abraham believed the Lord, and he (God) credited it to him as righteousness. Abram's name would not change to Abraham until the covenant of circumcision in chapter 17. There must have been long periods of time that would pass by between God meeting with Abram or speaking to him, enough for Abram's continence to change from hope to despair. Does that not sound like someone you know? We all become enamored with our circumstances at moments maybe for long periods. We forget what God has done for us or the prayers he has answered or the daily provisions he provides. Our barometer is off kilter we lose faith in what God can do.

We rely on our own resources to exist and we listen to people who don't know the Lord. I am certain this is what made Abram vulnerable through his life. This sheds great light on God's purpose in fleshing out Abram's lack of faith and unbelief at times. So if God knows all things from beginning to end why does he test Abram? God told Abram he was righteous, but then he chose to test his righteousness. God is omnipotent and omniscience, he has foreknowledge, and he has power, Abram I'm sure was perplexed when God commanded him to take his son Isaac up to the mountains of Moriah and offer him up to the Lord as a sacrifice. Recognizing the purpose for God's command is confusing and also sorrowful especially for Abram. Could we imagine the dreadful anguish that permeated through his soul and being during the journey to Moriah? Do we find ourselves walking the very same path to fulfill God's assignment at moments believing and rationalizing he doesn't really expect us to do what he asked of us? God serves his own purposes always for our well-being. Once again God is displaying his great patience, God needs no other proof of Abram's allegiance to him he knows all things he simply wanted to strengthen Abram's faith once again reassuring him that his destiny and unique purpose were still in place and for him to celebrate and execute his gift and life.

JEPHTHAH'S DAUGHTER

In the book of Judges chapter 11, we read about Jephthah's vow. There is great discussion about this story. We don't know the name of his daughter regardless this story has confused and bewildered people of the faith for some time. I would first like to address the most common belief that Jephthah's vow is believed by many to be nothing more than a human sacrifice, offering his daughter to the Lord if the Lord would deliver the Ammonites into his hands. I believe the spirit of the Lord moved Jephthah to make this vow. I believe he himself would not make a vow of this magnitude knowing the tradition of the Israelite women. This story in my opinion is more about God's plan and purpose for Jephthah's daughter than for giving him victory over his enemies.

Once again, this was an offering of dedication to the Lord just like Aaron and his sons the Levites (Leviticus 8) where dedicated by Moses. My understanding of this situation is clear after much study. God wants Jephthah to dedicate his daughter to himself. This is one part of the process the Lord is using to accomplish his plan for Jephthah's daughter's destiny and unique gift. Many people forget the Mosaic Law and commandments had been written and practiced long before Jephthah made this vow, therefore it would have been strictly forbidden to sacrifice humans in Israel, and he was a judge he would know the law better than anyone surely the vow was not referring to human sacrifice. He was simply proclaiming that whatever or whoever came out first to greet him that which did was to be offered up to the Lord as a sacrificial offering. It was customary in ancient Israel for the women to run out first to greet the fighting men and sing and shout for their victory and celebrate. I do realize some animals can run faster than humans and possible get out first although, we have no knowledge of any sort of animal in the house.

So in this case, Jephthah's daughter rushed out ahead of everyone. One can read this story and accept it as a tragedy or one can see the compelling truth, God had a plan for Jephthah's daughter from before the moment of her birth to the present. In her eyes in her anguish as an Israelite woman to be devoted to service to God for her entire life would manifest in having no husband and no children she would be a virgin forever. It was considered a curse to these people not having a family was crushing. This is a compelling story but, perhaps the real truth here is, she was special, and God knew this and he chose her to be his only for his service. Just like Enoch, Noah, or Elijah all of the great prophets. God revealed to her, her special unique gift her life purpose designed only for her. She mourned for two months with her friends knowing she would never marry or have children; however I believe once she realized her great purpose in life she would be overjoyed with gladness. We could say this is one of the first examples of women becoming as the nuns of the holy Catholic Church, or a foreshadow of the beginnings of the nunnery, this is purely my own speculation. Once she understands her significance and value to the Lord her mourning will turn to joy! She will exist for the soul purpose of glorifying God. To know or have first person knowledge of your unique purpose is to be blessed. To know what the potter designed the pottery for is to be blessed. Jephthah accomplished God's plan and purpose in his time, Jesus even spoke of his greatness, he is one of the great ones and so is his daughter. They are special vessels.

Note: What could be the reason why we are not given the name of Jephthah's daughter? The text reveals that she is his only offspring, why the Lord chose not to share this with the reader is somewhat perplexing. Like the unknown soldier's grave. No one knows who you are except God. Devoted to your creator and known only by him.

KING NEBUCHADNEZZAR

How often do we reflect on our circumstances and look with pride on all we have, we may have a nice home with a swimming pool in the backyard. We may have a three car garage and parked inside we gaze at our prized automobiles. Maybe we own a classic car, or a hotrod, or a convertible sports car. We may have a speedboat or recreational vehicle (RV), nothing but the best, for the best, really? We may even own a summer home on a lake somewhere, or on the ocean, or a cabin in the wilderness. Our bank accounts are huge and unlimited compared to our wants and desires. We never hold back when it comes to spending money on vacations or cars or gadgets, our lust for more motivates our actions to get more. Your life is the best you have it all, everything that satisfies is at your disposal your greater than all your neighbors, you're a king. This is the way it was for King Nebuchadnezzar. He was very proud and boisterous for all his accomplishments, "by my mighty power and for the glory of my majesty"? (Daniel 4:30) and at the beginning of the verse he says; "Is not this the great Babylon I have built as the royal residence." How long are we willing to follow in king Nebuchadnezzar's footsteps? You may not even recognize the symptoms of your illness until it's too late. Take a step back and analyze your situation. Your leaves have been stripped away and you never knew it. Your fruit fell to the ground and is beginning to rot around your feet in this moment. All the birds and animals have abandoned you and your branches have been cut off. Your stump has been trimmed down to the roots and you were unaware of it. You are a dead tree remaining in the ground, dead. You are a wild beast bound with iron and bronze. How long will you wonder back and forth on a chain, with the grass of the field in your mouth. Day and night you move and live among the animals and with the plants of the earth?

You're not even aware that you have the mind of a wild animal, so you inhabit the wilderness drenched with the dew of the heavens. In time you begin to resemble a wild animal, your hair grows long and tangled like an oxen and your nails grow dreadfully long and sharp as the claws of a African lion. How long will you dwell in this state? Seven hours seven days, seven years? It took seven years in order for king Nebuchadnezzar to be humbled and his sanity to be restored. It's been said doing the same thing over and over and getting the same result but expecting new results is called insanity I think? Pull it together humble yourself like the king of Babylon before God humbles you, and save yourself all the trouble, humble yourself before the Lord and worship him and only him.

AUNT HAZEL

Today, my wife and I went to my aunt's funeral. I was honored to be a pallbearer for her. My aunt loved everyone, she raised five children, weathered two divorces, and she was a repair woman for everyone. She mended buttons. She loved loving people. She worked as a waitress for many years up to the age of seventy eight years old. She loved waiting on people serving human beings, I don't know whether she knew this was her purpose in life or not but she was good at it. She lived through the great depression, lived amid poverty and hard times, but she always had a smile on her face and a kind word to say to you. Hazel may very well have been an angel here on earth, she never longed to be somewhere else or, be consumed with dreams of a better life for herself. She was always content to be there for her family to encourage and support them. I can ascertain from my view of her life she knew this to be her purpose and gift from God even though she never proclaimed it. Once again we learn that the great potter of the universe molds his creation gently and delicately into vessels for grand or honorable uses and some vessels for common task.

Perhaps we miss the real point here; there is a different insight to this, my aunt's purpose in life seems quite insignificant and rather ordinary, but perhaps in the sight of God she was a grand vessel one that shined bright, one that was his most wonderful creation in which brought him tremendous glory and joy. "The last will be first and the first shall be last" (Matthew 20:16).

WASTED TIME

Why would God waste his time reaching out to rebellious people? He sees their rebellion here on earth; will they be any different when they enter eternity? Pursuing one's own interest is outright rebellion against God. To become self-sufficient and independent is rebellion. If people want nothing to do with God here and now, if they have no time to spend nurturing a close relationship with him or his son or his spirit here during this earthly existence, then why do we assume they will change when they are in his presence face-to-face someday? People want it all; we believe we can possess everything this world has to offer and then some. And we believe we can have even more when we get to eternity. We are certain we are wise beyond our time; man's perception of himself is blasphemy to God. Men will always spend excessive amounts of time and energy and effort in order to disprove God's wisdom and this is sin in its truest most basic form: pride. The wisdom of man is foolishness to God. I've heard it all my life, don't be afraid to be curious, question everything, explore, be adventurous.

This wisdom is interesting and peculiar yet, this is exactly what compelled Satan long ago. Man has tried to dress it up, make it more palatable somewhat acceptable, it has taken a long time to accomplish but now it no longer needs to be camouflaged in order to be displayed, it is the wisdom of the times. It has once been said by a renowned theologian that "hell was created for the overly curious." Absolute trust and obedience to God's word and Holy Spirit once again is the anecdote.

Confused and dismayed maybe we perceive with a heart out of focus, blurred vision, perhaps the ordinary is not so ordinary. It may very well be something opposite, somewhat hidden, subtle, discrete but directly before our eyes yet invisible. The obvious doesn't always manifest. We need to practice holding a keen site line; this will not take place under the influence of the flesh. This insight will only come from the power of the Holy Spirit. This too is only allowed by God's providence (Ephesians 1:4–14, Galatians 4:6–7, 5:13–25). God may be lovingly shielding us from viewing our future, or perhaps placing hurdles in our path for the soul purpose of strengthening our faith and increasing our patience. Let me demonstrate this idea; perhaps some of us stay on the potter's wheel most if not all of our lives; some spend less time on it than others, but those who stay on it for an extended period, stay unfinished vessels, still in the making, God has not yet determined when you will be a finished vessel ready for the furnace.

Once the vessel is created, it is ready for the furnace (kiln) to be fired, then its destiny is sealed for its entire life. The potter has sealed the fate of his creation. The piece of pottery will only be useful for what it was made to do. The creation cannot change its purpose or design no matter how compelled it may be whether for honorable purposes or common uses. He may very well be waiting for a certain point in time to secure your destiny. Can we recognize this moment in our lives? Do we realize how God refines our character leading us toward completion to be put to the fire? Who we are and who we want to be or think we should be are valid and important questions that deserve insightful thought.

"Trust in the Lord and do good; dwell in the land and enjoy safe pasture. Delight yourself in the Lord and he will give you the desires of your heart. Commit your way to the Lord; trust in him and he will do this: He will make your righteousness shine like the dawn, the justice of your cause like the noonday sun. Be still before the Lord and wait patiently for him" (Psalms 37:3–7).

"Commit to the Lord whatever you do, and your plans will succeed" "In his heart a man plans his course, but the Lord determines his steps" (Proverbs 16:3–9).

ROADS, HUMANS, FENCES

Will each person stay on the road they receive from the moment of their existence? Only God has that knowledge where that road may end. Each person will end up somewhere we don't know; well we can ascertain a few truths from looking at some folk's lifestyle. The desires and interest of each individual play a key role for determining their road. Their road may have detours at times but most people will never choose a different road.

After a while, maybe a few years it becomes so routine and comfortable and safe, not to mention the familiarity of the scenery is satisfying they feel secure, similar to my pet dog. She has been in our backyard her whole life from the time she was six weeks old. She has spent her entire life behind a white picket fence, I never let her out of the fenced backyard mostly because we live on a major highway and I didn't want her wandering onto it for her protection from possible injury from cars. She feels safe and secure behind the picket fence but as soon as you pick her up and take her out of the backyard she becomes afraid and fearful and begins to shake and pant, she can't do anything else. Are we humans just like my dog at moments in our life? What would compel us to try another road, what would motivate our being to take action? Does God know who can and cannot adjust their habits and life when their environment changes, take another road? Does he plan this in every human being or does he inject it into only a certain number of souls? God only and he alone can know the life and destiny of all human beings. I know in my life I have not received any one specific assignment from God.

Yes, I know we are to nurture the gifts of the spirit which I continue to practice, but I have found no one certain tailor made job from God strictly for me. I have become a "jack of all trades" so to speak. This resembles my employment history. This is not a negative thing it has been very useful in supporting my family. My motto has always been; "a man needs to be versatile to make a living." Having multiple skills is invaluable in the workplace. You and your family will never go hungry, and you will never be without work. I am certain this is a gift from God. In our churches I believe this to be true also, God's intentions are to teach and train each one of his children in many different areas of service and stewardship throughout their lives', instead of specialized training in one specific role or job title, I'm mostly referring to jobs in his church but this should spill over into each individuals personal life and work setting. There are many different occupations that require many types of skill sets where each person has the opportunity to use their gifts and talents. In one of the earlier chapters I spoke about the many areas where I have served in the Lord's church, I was amazed at times, how the Lord refined some of my old gifts when I thought they were of no more use to me in my ministry but how I was mistaken. "Trust in the Lord with all your heart and lean not on your own understanding; in all your ways acknowledge him, and he will make your paths straight" (Proverbs 3:5–6).

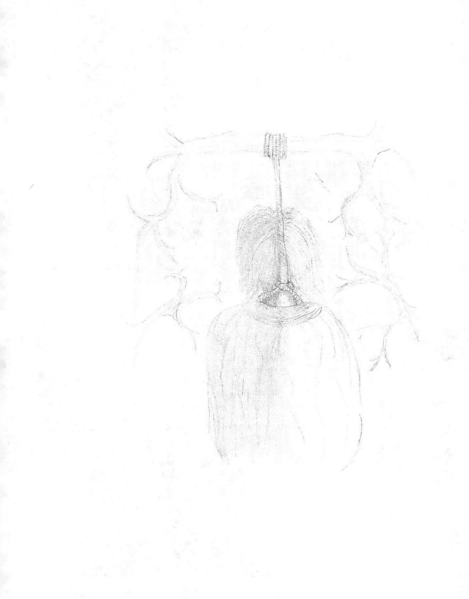

JUDAS ISCARIOT

He was the treasurer; he was the holder of the money bag. Down through the centuries he has been portrayed as a demon or the devil himself. Jesus chose him to be one of his disciples. I want to look at this appointment for Judas somewhat closer. Was Judas doomed from birth; was he marked for this purpose from before the moment of his conception? Jesus said, "One of you will betray me but woe to that man, it would be better for that man not to have been born." How could Judas be the only soul sufficient for recruitment for this purpose? Someone would need to be the betrayer but why should it be one of Jesus's disciples his students? Perhaps this was planned from the beginning in the garden that, Judas Iscariot would be that doomed soul. Was this a foreordained conclusion, did the potter create this vessel exclusively to execute this task, for a specific moment in space time, Chronos time, to bring to completion his purpose our savior's betrayal and he knew it not.

We have always had the mind-set and been educated that this was a despicable offense that happened to Jesus, although taking a closer look we can find irony here. The betrayal was significant in that for Jesus to be arrested it needed to happen, so then the events that are crucial to our salvation can take place fulfilling prophecy. Jesus then can clothe himself with the punishment that we deserve and pay the penalty or price for our salvation on the cross. This betrayal was paramount, it was pivotal to God's whole plan and process for our redemption, and I truly believe Judas at some point watching these events unfold from beginning to end from the arrest to the crucifixion to the death of Jesus realized he made a terrible mistake and I believe he felt greatly responsible for the events that took place. Devastated and remorseful he returned the thirty pieces of silver to the Pharisees; he was compelled by his remorsefulness demonstrating his understanding of his actions. Judas truly had not exhibited any new actions that had not manifested in the other disciples through all the events that took place. In the story of Mary pouring the expensive nard onto Jesus feet we know from one of the gospel accounts there were other disciples who were indignant about Mary wasting the pure nard Judas was indeed not the only protester. Peter disowned Jesus three times and vehemently at that, in the presence of many people. The remaining disciples with the exception of John abandoned Jesus, ran, and went into hiding. I don't know if Judas was present while Jesus explained to them that the son of man would have to suffer and die then be raised to life on the third day.

Assuming he was there then he should have had hope, hope that Jesus would forgive him for his betrayal. Scripture says Judas went and hung himself, probably before Jesus was resurrected. I'm speculating but I believe Judas may have been so overwhelmed with shame and hopelessness, with no way to undo what had been done, he convinced himself he was not loved by God or Jesus but doomed to destruction and rejection now knowing fully his true purpose for living. Judas reasoned in his mind he could not return to the disciples especially Peter, without them disowning him. They all knew he was the reason for Jesus's arrest and ultimately his death and they would hate him for it. They knew his character and his actions; he always moved in the shadows and took money for himself from the money bag. They were fully aware of his deceitfulness and habits. I wonder if Jesus knew in his heart Judas would give up in the end.

Jesus mentored him for three years alongside the other disciples in the same settings same places same miracles. Why would it take all the events to come to full completion for Judas's eyes to be opened, the question still remains in my mind; was this Judas's purpose and destiny? My response: only God knows. Are we not like Judas in our existence, do we despair sometimes about our disloyalty to God we betray him over and over again and again like a record player skipping. We then tell ourselves he must love me less or not at all because I am such a dastardly person. We anguish over our failures and adversity, mixed with sorrow and contempt. Our reaction to these elements is the key here; we have an example from the previous paragraph the right response is needed, not self-pity but repentance. Like the dog who returns to his vomit, or the sow who returns to her wallow, we return to our shame. Like a familiar pair of shoes, how they feel so good the fit is perfect and they are comfortable.

We are determined to feel safe and secure even if we abandon our God. Peter was a good example of this; after the crucifixion and everything had settled down he returned to his familiar way of life fishing. He began to rebuild his fishing career, but I don't believe he abandoned his God. He immersed himself into the vocation he felt safe and secure in before he left to follow Jesus for three years. I will speculate once more here wondering what would Peter's reaction be if Judas had not hung himself but decided to seek out Peter and the remaining disciples longing for their forgiveness and restoration, and wanting to be reinstated as one of the twelve. We all long for restoration and its well within our reach each and every day. "I call on the Lord and he answers me" (Psalms 120:1).

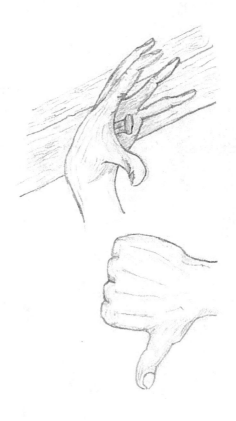

GOD'S LOVE AND REJECTION

Does God love some people more than others; perhaps his love, in one way is similar to the air we breathe, it permeates the earth within the atmosphere constant, and providing the key elements for organisms to live and thrive. Ultimately everything that needs it will not live without it according to the love of God. He has made provisions for all life each living creature but will this change one day, will his love be exclusive some day? One day, the wheat will be separated from the chaff. One day the rapture will take place, one day the dead will rise, one day Jesus will return, who will rise to life everlasting and who will rise to damnation is not known but will the love of God be different, will it change during this moment in time? Will God mourn over the damned and lost? Most people advocate that God is love rather than any other attribute which couldn't be further from the truth. Some people, mostly from the secular world are convinced that somehow God will be compelled to increase the measure of his love and mercy for mankind mostly for those who are not saved at the end of time, and decrease the measure of justice and punishment.

Oddly enough even some Christians have embraced this train of thought, they focus on the scripture, which says, "God is love." Yes, he is love but he is also just and holy and lives in unapproachable light. God is also an angry God to those who have rejected him, and his love. We all know what rejection feels like. All people are familiar with rejection in some way shape or form and so is God. Before the beginning God was rejected by Lucifer and hundreds of thousands of angels so he removed them from his presence, God loved Lucifer tremendously, it has been said he was the most beautiful angel of them all. Frankly speaking who would not believe God would not have the right to do the same with all those souls who have come and gone through time who, even though they were good people they neither acknowledged him as God or worshiped him but lived their lives for themselves.

God is accountable for his actions to himself only. He needs to give no explanation for his thoughts and plans to anyone. His motives are his alone to achieve. He chooses to include humans in his eternal plan to be part of his blueprint. He has confirmed a place for us in his marvelous "Kairos" he wants to partner with his chosen children. He sends his spirit wondering to and fro on the earth gathering his elect those who are receptive to his call. Those who are his elect are foreordained from the beginning to be children of the living God. God is omnipotent; he knows the state of every human beings heart, those who will receive him and those who will reject him. The obligation of the elect is to do the will of God. Not for salvation but from a deep, deep gratitude for the unexplainable for the immeasurable love and mercy and grace that God has covered us with. We are held accountable to God and to ourselves He commands us to "be holy as I am holy." This is not optional, the spirit will empower us to achieve this, and we should endeavor to cultivate a willing heartbroken contrite, and pliable heart.

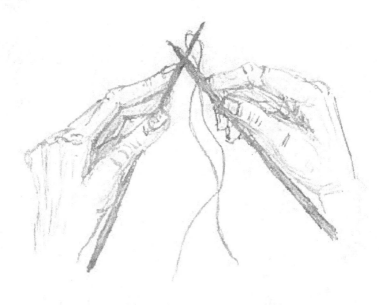

GRANDMOTHERS

I wrote previously in a chapter regarding my Catholic grandmother who was a devout one at that rich in mercy and good works. My other grandmother on my mother's side of our family was not so fortunate or blessed. My grandfather divorced her long before I was old enough to know what divorce was about. My grandmother was very poor; she lived on welfare for quite some time. She lived in humble rental units which were not to appealing. My grandmother on my father's side was always checking on my grandmother from my mom's side. She could still drive so she was much more independent than my mom's mom. She would frequently visit her.

Then one day, my grandmother, my mom's mom had a fall and never walked again. She spent the rest of her life in the nursing home about fifteen years or so. She then developed Parkinson's disease. After a while the disease progressed and took my grandmothers speech and her motor skills. She was mostly paralyzed. The only thing she could do when she had visitors was cry, very sad. I have often wondered what the purpose was for her to suffer like that. What was her gift from God, her uniqueness why was she left in that nursing home mute and motionless to suffer? "He forgives our sins and heals all our diseases" (Psalms 103:3).

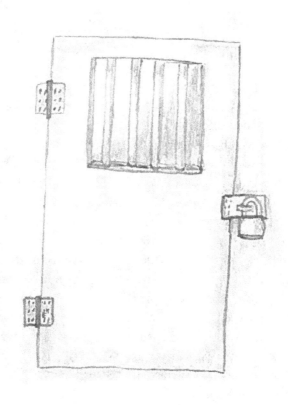

WRONGFUL CONVICTIONS

Here sits a man in prison behind thick concrete walls one little porthole window for a view. Cold steel bars to hold onto. Convicted of a crime he didn't commit. He's been imprisoned for twenty one years. Someone once asked him if he wanted to be let out and his reply was "Yes, but I wouldn't know where to go or what to do." Where would I begin he replied, how to start over or where to begin, I don't know was his answer. Living again on the outside is frightening to say the least. Someone else asked him if he was innocent of the crime he is accused of committing. "Yes I am" was his response emphatically. He was quick to say, "though I am innocent I've spent twenty-one years in here I believe this is where I'm supposed to be. My life is coming to an end and I know this is my destiny. I have fought with depression and defeated it; I've put to bed the anxiety that haunted me for many sleepless nights. I buried the resentment that suffocated me every day. I'm free now; I'm content now to be where I am. No more yearning to be vindicated for crimes I didn't commit, it doesn't matter anymore."

What would it take for each one of us to come to a place where this man has ended up, I'm not referring to being in prison, but complete surrender to God, "Not my will, Lord, but yours be done, amen." Since we're on the subject of prison or incarceration, let's discuss the despicable. Are murderers on God's list of chosen people? What about child molesters? How about serial killers? There is a multitude of questions regarding these monsters. More often than not we assume these people are counted out of election. Though they are being punished for their crimes they may even be on death roll, their wickedness and dastardly deeds are being paid for here on earth suffering the consequences for their actions. But is this their purpose their destiny, God's plan for their existence, how could their actions glorify God.

They are the scum of the earth, unforgiven and abandoned, thrown away by humanity marked for disposal. Believe it or not some may even be children of God, chosen for this specific destiny to glorify him in prison to witness for him. Providence at work wherever Yahweh determines according to his time and space, and people arriving at their destiny. Even though they will never be welcomed back into society some will be welcomed into eternity as God's elect "today you will be with me in paradise" (Luke 23:43).

MEMORIES AND HEAVEN

Heaven will be tearless, painless, no grief, God will wipe them all away. Will we have memories of loved ones lost in eternity. Family members who perished for their unbelief, stubborn, rebellious, and defiant, unwilling to turn to God. Lost friends who lived for pleasure and self. People who chose the world over the gift of salvation. How will we be cleansed from the agony we carry from the memories of these people? The sorrow and grief that plague our minds here on earth. Will we carry these with our being into heaven, how will Jesus accomplish this, what will be the process?

The book of Revelation says all things will be made new. I assume this to mean even our hearts and memories will be refreshed, not reconditioned but rebuilt new for eternity. I understand this concept little, though I have hope and assurance this will come to fruition just as the author of revelation has predicted. Some speculate the book of Revelation to be mostly metaphors and prophetic in content, I am apprehensive to believe this, perhaps it does reveal volumes concerning God's plan for the inhabitants of the earth. I'd rather believe this instead. Some, however, would chastise me for wading too far out into the water. Perhaps I'm discussing and pondering things that are dangerous and confusing, is it forbidden to search the mind of our God; If we worship him, we want to fellowship with him, we should be consumed with knowing him, this includes all areas of his character and intentions. I still want to investigate this more. God will not make clones, he will not create robots, even in the age to come. He gave free will to humans that being said, will we have the capacity to remember all the lost souls from the former life of sin?

All those from every area of our lives who refused the free gift of salvation, those who ignored the spirits call. Perhaps we will be reprogrammed to forget the former things. The pain and sorrow, regret, and mourning will just be deleted by the press of a button. Or suddenly those sad memories will be blurred and begin to dim and as time goes by they continue to progress until they have completely vanished. Or maybe the great joy of being in the marvelous presence of our Lord will extinguish all those negative emotions and memories. We will be transformed into God's righteousness holy and dearly loved. The great I Am will precipitate all filth and negative remains of the curse from our beings. What will we experience on that day, what it might be compared to when the pressure that holds us down is lifted from our souls. He who is seated on the throne said, "I am making everything new!" Then he said, "Write this down, for these words are trustworthy and true" (Revelation 21:5).

SEARCHING

I'm not a theologian. I'm not a prophet. I'm not a Bible scholar. I'm not a pastor. I don't possess a PhD or doctorate in biblical theology, but what I am is one of the numerous unfortunate souls who has been kept in suspense my entire life regarding my vocation or occupation. I do believe part of our uniqueness and gift is meant for social service, that which we could offer to society to better or improve the lives of people who are less fortunate than most people. How do we discover these things, how do we go on without losing hope? Life is brief but a breath.

I constantly think about the remaining time I have left of my existence, this inhabits my mind and thoughts more frequently as I continue to age. Day after day, I become more and more anxious for I realize I'm running out of time. It becomes more precious as we have less I now understand this. It's urgent to complete the task and purpose or plans mapped out for me. Therefore we should always endeavor to be searchers of God's plan for our lives. Also, I see things changing rapidly, my mind is becoming less sharp, my physical strength and energy is depleting. No one can conquer the law of decay. During these moments of evaluation and conclusions I choose to think like Solomon and read his wisdom. "He who pursues righteousness and love finds life, prosperity and honor." "There is a way that seems right to a man but in the end it leads to death." "Many are the plans in a man's heart, but it is the Lords' purpose that prevails" (Proverbs 21:21, Proverbs 16:25, Proverbs 19:21) be searchers always!

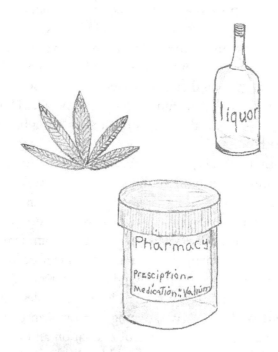

WORRY, FEAR, ANXIETY

I am a worrywart, I must confess; I have nervous energy. When I was a boy, I would pace back and forth through the rooms of our tiny house. I learned to worry from an early age. My mother was a great teacher on how to worry. Fear is the fruit of worry, when we feed on fear it digests into anxiety; it will rot in your stomach. When we feel those butterflies in our gut this is the symptom of anxiety. We cannot let these demons make their home in our soul. These dreadful entities saturate my life all because I am uncertain if I am in the place where God needs me. Ultimately I keep telling myself there is no confirmation from him. These insecurities are alive and well simply from the doubt in my mind haunting me and debating with my consciousness every day, asking me, "are you where God wants you? Are you doing what God wants you to do? Are you serving where God wants you to serve? Are you in the occupation God designed you to do? Are you doing the right things? Are you praying the right prayers? Are you asking for the right things or wrong things?"

Worry and its cohorts inspire us to question God's goodness and provisions. When I became a Christian, I had hope and belief God would reveal my vocation to me, partly because I still had many years in front of me to work. So I was certain I needed just to be patient. Suddenly now I'm nearing retirement and now I'm even more uncertain about this, have I been in a place where he has planned for me to be? I know his plans cannot be thwarted by anyone or anything. Though I fail to understand the reasons he is hiding these things from my vision. I know there are many people who are familiar with these same thoughts. Scripture says these struggles and trials are meant to help us grow. Regardless of where I have been or where I should have been, through all the worry and fear and anxiety God still provided for me and my family. During this time of provision I was working to discover my destiny mostly my vocation using my own power and will. This was all in vain; instead I should have called on God.

See, I was so consumed with the present I forgot about the journey, God will lead us if we would just follow. Faith overcomes worry, fear, anxiety, searching for his plan is simple; spend time getting to know him. Even though I can say I am in the dark about my place in this world prepared for me, God is still working to prepare me for it someday. So returning to our struggle with worry, fear and anxiety, what will it take to reprogram our mind, our brain, our soul, our emotions, and our view of life with our circumstances? Let me explain, worry, fear, and anxiety are products of our fallen sin nature. Fear, once fully matured, produces fruit—anxiety. These demons can be difficult to conquer. I lived as a child growing into an adult where worry was cultivated daily. I'm not in any way making excuses for myself for living in a secular home, this was common. We all know social environments play a key role in child development. I believe God can change me, I believe this and it is possible. If we ask and seek he will hand us the necessary tools required to achieve this goal. These elements, tormenters of our soul are debilitating and we need to believe with the power of God we will overcome these demons. Scripture is clear, we can be victorious over these weaknesses, we can live with power, we can live victorious, and we can learn that we can change our view. We need to ask and be patient and humbly get rid of pride, dispose of it, throw it in the trash, burn it in the fireplace. "Seek the Lord with all your heart and lean not on your own understanding."

When you recognize the signs of uncertainty returning with its train of worry and fear and anxiety following, stop, take a step back and go to the word of God and dwell in his presence and on his promises. His word is a powerful weapon for his children. "Do not be anxious about anything, but by prayer and petition, with thanksgiving, present your request to God" (Philippians 4:6).

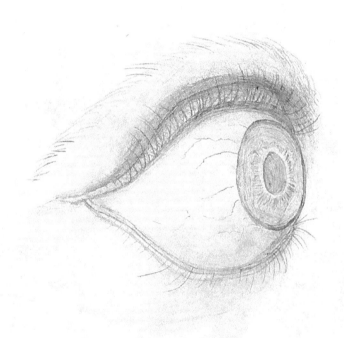

VISION

Sometimes our view of life may be obscured, narrow or blurred. Maybe we only see part of the picture or of the landscape. Our view perhaps might well be filtered from unknown causes. Due to numerous distractions we may have tunnel vision. However, our own perception of life may be the cause of this blindness. Unaware of this it may be God who is the answer to our limited vision. He may give us only a glimpse at certain moments. This brings me to remember to live from moment to moment, be patient this is a process and that's okay. Remember you are a work in progress, he knows you will only be able to handle so much. This gives me a great piece of mind, he's in control and all I have to do is focus my vision on communion with him, this is most valuable, for I can see clearly now.

When I began writing this book, my main goal was to create something that would inspire and motivate people to search out the living God. And also with that to seek and search for the true reason for their existence not what they imagine it to be, but to discover what God created them to be. I wanted to share my struggles and failures and my victories and to encourage everyone so they know they're not alone in their walk. Alienation can be exhausting and despair is consuming. Once again I must repeat myself, this is his will for our lives like it or not, he is compelled and determined to refine our beings, he will not abandon his creations. One last thing, there are mysteries beyond our capacity to comprehend, the reason for this is our dreadful sinful nature, it is the barrier. Will God be disgusted with his children for exploring these issues; perhaps he would rather want us to focus our energies on more important truths? Ultimately in the end, I believe he gives us permission to explore these mysteries keeping him first always. For further study, we can also go to other sources such as; literature from the great thinkers from the first century to the reformation, two thousand years' worth of valuable information from many theologians.

Also there are plenty of resources available to study the ancient writings as well as many different Bible interpretations. We have the advantage and luxury to have access to these incredible documents. They can be very helpful in applying them to our journeys through our lives, though we should be cautious when studying these writings, with sincerity and humbleness asking God to guide us. We do have one thing that is for sure, one thing that we all know will take place at some moment in each of our lives. Determining the exact moment this thing will happen we do not know. We have no information regarding the date or time it will be here. It will come upon some swiftly others not so swiftly, and some perhaps may see warning signs early on before it happens. However, it could very well show up tomorrow or the next day for some folks or even this moment. We may not recognize it, mostly because we don't know what to look for then suddenly there it is. We have never experienced it so we have no idea what it feels like.

Probably the answer for this is clear, we all will only experience this once here on earth, and this is the common theme. This is the part of our destiny which we all share; we may have many different purposes and gifts each with their own uniqueness and special talents for their vocation but the one thing we will all accomplish according to the final part of our destiny to bring it to completion is our death. One last thought, what would you do with your life right now if you were given the exact month, day and year of your death down to the hour and minute.

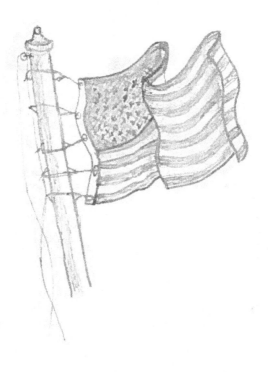

FREEDOM

W hat if God gave every individual the freedom to choose for themselves the path of their life and their choice of employment? What would this be like, why would he stop there, he could let them choose every little detail of their life. The power to choose everything we feel we need. Would this not be catastrophic, think about it? The power to choose every detail, let me demonstrate; let's say when you were born your God given destiny was to be a car, but when you became an adult ready to move into the workplace you decided you wanted to fly, when you were a little boy that was all you dreamed about was flying high above the clouds. How difficult it became for you in your occupation when you discovered you didn't have the knowledge or talents or gifts to do your job, you can't fly. This story is filled with some humor but sadly this is true for millions of lost souls. Actually God has already written our story from before we were born.

Now some folks would speak up and say then we don't have free will. My response to this statement is yes, God gives us the freedom to make choices but these choices are always within the confines of his will. In the end, God's plan and purposes will come to completion. Now I want to give you an account of a true experience. A quick look at my early life. In a previous chapter, I spoke of the heroes in my life which my childhood buddies and myself idolized and wanted to be just like them. They were professional football players from many different teams, keep in mind this was the end of the 1960s and early to mid-seventies. I loved football and from that time on I knew what I wanted to be when I grew up, a professional football player. This was my dream for many years. Even after my graduation from high school I was sure this was my destiny. Ultimately I never received any offers with scholarship money available from colleges wanting me to play football for them. I did receive offers to come and play but none with financial help. I did receive one letter of intent from Cornel University which gave me hope, and flattered me immensely but I couldn't meet the grade point requirement. I was a great player though not outstanding enough to catch the eye of scouts who could recommend me for scholarships.

So I went to college and was recruited by the track coach mainly due to my pole vaulting skills. The next year, I dropped out of college mostly for financial reasons and also I had really no idea what I should study. I wanted to play football, that was my dream and I had a passion in my gut to do so. I was devastated when it looked as though it would not happen. So I decided to get a job and go to work not knowing what I should do, what kind of work should I do, what am I good at, I had no idea what God wanted me to do. Then a few years later, I began playing on a semi-pro team. I made the all-star team after my first year of play but in my third year I suffered a career ending injury and I never played again. Unfortunately, this unknown knowledge of my vocation has driven the cycle of my employment history. I have worked in many different vocations not knowing if they were what I was designed to do. How do we overcome broken dreams and haunting regrets? "Many are the plans in a man's heart, but it is the Lord's purpose which prevails" (Proverbs 19:21).

LUCIFER

Not much has been written about Satan or should I say regarding his time before his fall from heaven. There is only the scriptures to depend on and maybe some folklore available down through time; therefore, I want to go deeper, and contemplate, mostly speculate concerning God's plan for Satan, his original purpose and design he envisioned in his mind for this being named "Lucifer." Lucifer, the angel of light was the most beautiful angel in heaven so we are told. He shined brilliantly in heaven brighter than all the other angels. This curiosity has compelled me to dig deeper, to investigate. This desire to know more may plunge us where we should not be it can be dangerous. We must take warning not to assume things that may not be fact, the scriptures are somewhat vague and short in context concerning Satan and what has been written and reported about him.

So let's begin, If God had foreknowledge, a vision of the future which illustrated who Lucifer would become, all the dreadful actions and evil that he would spread through time, starting with the rebellion in heaven why did God decide to give him life? Remember God is omnipotent and omniscience. There was a great battle in heaven that took place, Lucifer and one third of the angels failed in their effort to dethrone God. God, therefore, had no other option but to banish Lucifer and the angels who followed him. These angels preferred to become demons shedding their heavenly robes to follow Satan into the darkness. God might have saved himself and mankind many sorrows and anguish if he would have refrained himself from creating this being destined for hell. We know from scripture in the book of Genesis God still had communication with Satan after the rebellion. He cursed him in the Garden of Eden; he made a wager with him in the book of Job regarding Job's commitment to God.

God gave Satan permission to return to his throne to speak with him on occasion, in the book of Job 1:6, Satan presents himself to the Lord along with the angels. Satan explains to God he has come from roaming the earth to and fro. Jesus speaks of seeing Satan fall like lighting from heaven; therefore we know he was removed by God.

We know he was banished to the earth according to the books of Genesis and Job and the Gospels. And so this says something about God's character, He will change his actions depending on the actions of his creations at any moment, if he so chooses. Jesus also conversed with Satan in the desert during his forty days of purification and temptation as well as some of the demons or evil spirits, or fallen angels which he encountered throughout the gospels. So this is my personal theory confronting this situation; maybe if Satan had a change of heart, and recognized the harm he has inflicted on God and the angels and mankind, and suddenly discovered his need for God once more, could this happen? Satan would need to go to God in heaven, and present himself to the Lord in order to enter the throne room. Satan then would need to repent and plead for forgiveness acknowledging the seriousness and capacity of his actions and become humble and contrite. This is purely speculation and analytical thought on my part, I truly don't believe Satan has the capacity to change, he has fallen so far into lasciviousness and depravity it would take a miracle from God.

However, I believe God could change his actions surrounding Satan's dilemma. God may perhaps make provisions for forgiveness and restoration. Remember this is purely imagination and speculation on my part, there is no proof supporting this theory. I just want to try to understand more about God's original purpose for Satan and if his being is salvageable, or should I say does God believe, or know this to be true. Let me explain; in the book of Jeremiah 18:2–10; this is God speaking to Jeremiah, "Go down to the potter's house and there I will give you my message." So I went down to the potter's house, and I saw him working at the wheel. But the pot he was shaping from the clay was marred and blemished in his hands; so the potter formed it into another pot, shaping it as seemed best to him. Then the word of the Lord came to me: "O house of Israel, can

I not do with you as this potter does?" declares the Lord. "Like clay in the hand of the potter, so are you in my hand, O house of Israel. If at any time I announce a nation or kingdom is to be uprooted, torn down and destroyed, and if that nation I warned repents of its evil, then I will relent and not inflict on it the disaster I had planned. And if at another time I announce that a nation or kingdom is to be built up and planted, and if it does evil in my sight and does not obey me, then I will reconsider the good I had intended to do for it."

I'm not advocating for new theology here, however, anything is possible with our God. He can change the condition of anyone's heart if he so chooses to, even Satan's. There are numerous scripture verses supporting this in regard to the heart of man. The heart of man is the home where his character dwells. Angels and demons, I have little to no information or hard data to establish a firm conclusion as to the substance of their heart, whether it is similar to men or not. Proverbs 4:23 tells us, "The heart of man is likened to a wellspring or cistern," or maybe a large storage tank in which his thoughts feelings emotions and actions and his entire decision making are stored and flow from. But then in the book of Jeremiah 17:9 we read, "The heart is deceitful above all things and beyond cure." We humans are incapable of truly knowing how sinful our hearts are, and what about Satan's heart? Can he recognize how dastardly his heart really is, how sinful he has become in his current state? Just like mankind it will take divine intervention revelation and conviction, before he would acknowledge his complete depravity.

Finally, I believe we can conclude God will react accordingly in response to human actions and to Satan's as well. This brings me back to the question I started with, the purpose and plan for Lucifer's existence. He was created with remarkable gifts and beauty which he forfeited for independence which manifested in failing to fulfill God's assignment gifted to him. Does this not sound familiar? This earth was created good and beautiful, but now after the curse, the devil has claimed it for his kingdom, it is his domain, his palace. On the contrary, everything he imagined and wanted takes place here, all his lust, his every desire, the freedom to sin and feed his giant ego. This was all created by him from the first time he sinned and rebelled. The first rebellion was orchestrated by him, Hostile to God, Satan, the God of this world of unbelieving lost sinners encourages his principles of greed, self-centeredness, pleasure, and ambition to all.

1 John 2:15–17 describes this as the lust of the flesh, the lust of the eyes, the pride of life, sensualism, worshiping counterfeit objects. Well, the magnitude of the damage is overwhelming, nevertheless does this shed light on the character of the former angel of light?

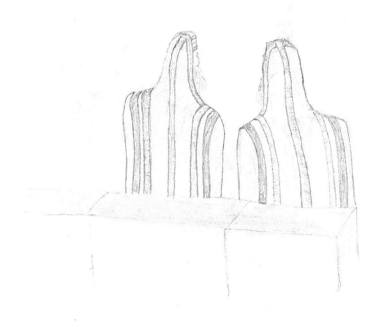

PHARISEES

As the religious leaders, priest and scribes of Israel, the Pharisees often suffered scathing rebuke and humiliation at the hands of Jesus on more than one occasion. There is a catalog of many confrontations in which Jesus really let them have it with both barrels. There was one exception to the rule, when Nicodemus came to him in the cool of the night. Reading the text it seems as though Jesus was more gentle and patient with him. However, Jesus still spoke to him in a mysterious manner. Nicodemus seemed confused, dull and slow to understand. Ultimately though in the end, after the crucifixion and death of Jesus I do believe Nicodemus's eyes were finally opened as well as Joseph of Arimathea to the truth and plan of God. They were secret followers, but now they were not afraid to show their faith at work. They no longer had to move and linger in the dark. They abandoned the fear that haunted them from secretly following Jesus. They now where brave and bold enough to show their willingness to worship and serve the Christ of Nazareth. We read no more of these two gentlemen once Jesus is buried in the tomb donated by Joseph of Arimathea. Were these things that took place the only purposes given to these men, surely not. I have no knowledge of the remaining days or years of these two Pharisees; therefore all I can do is speculate. Perhaps these two teachers were given new purposes, on the contrary maybe they will work behind the scenes, suppose God needs these two fellows to witness to some of the leaders of Israel, possibly implying, among this notorious gang of Jesus haters there is some who will be changed according to God's plan and purpose. Perhaps God knows there are some of his children among this group of self-righteous men. Are all the rest destined for damnation? Time will tell.

Did Jesus not know the destiny of the Pharisees and chief priest that ordered his death? What I'm trying to say is he did pray for them, on the cross he asked the father to forgive them for they know not what they do. Jesus loved everyone even those who despised him and wanted him dead. When he said this prayer to the father perhaps the word "they" is much more inclusive than we first imagined. Could it be Jesus was praying not only for the soldiers who hung him on that cross, those who spat on him, those who beat him, flogged him with a whip which was equipped with sharp fragments of bone and steel attached to each strand, put a crown of sharp thorns on his head and then they mocked him? No I believe he is also praying for those who wanted him dead.

The leaders of Israel, teachers of the law Caiaphas, and the chief priest, officers of the temple guard, remember he did heal the ear of Malchus the temple guard, the ruling council of the elders of the people; even Herod the Great and his guards mocked him and ridiculed him, even Simon from Cyrene contributed to his death. The centurion and Pilot and Pilot's wife may not have wanted Jesus to die, but fear persuaded them to turn their eyes away and look no more. Jesus prayed for mercy and forgiveness and salvation for these individuals all the while they were killing him, remarkable! Maybe among these people there is some who will have a different destiny and better purpose on their resume when they go before God, better than we concluded. Maybe after all is said and done just maybe, God will relent, and answer Jesus's prayer for mercy.

Remember even Jesus had mercy and pity for Malchus one of the temple guards who came to arrest him. Peter is said to have attacked him and sliced off his ear, suddenly Jesus picked up the ear and reattaches it to Malchus's head amazing, and this is Jesus. Everyone there is perplexed and astonished, including the guards. But they without fail continue with the assignment given to them by the religious leaders. Jesus chastised the Pharisees time and time again, calling them children of their father the devil, but on the cross he displays his love for them by declaring to the father that they are ignorant and unaware of their actions, please forgive them, have mercy on them, please offer them salvation; this is Jesus. So what is there that we can glean from these stories and truth given to us concerning these evil people who played a role in the greatest love story ever told? I struggle to locate any words in the English language, which would fully describe the depth and volume of these intangible qualities. The journey each of these people took after all that happened is a mystery, did these people eventually find their God given purpose, one that glorified him and served Jesus with the real skills God created them to use. If they were to look back at this moment in time would they have regret or satisfaction for their role in the things that took place?

JAMES

"Let's stop here and rest for a bit this is half way," James exclaimed. So I agreed, it hadn't been two minutes and to our surprise here came a big guy up the trail behind us, I don't know how he caught up to us so fast as we were traveling at a brisk pace. He was huffing and puffing packing only one fishing pole while I was packing my huge pack, which I use to spike camp and carry out big game if I happen to shoot something, but it was not hunting season. I was only trying to get in shape for the up and coming season. So was James, he was packing a smaller pack himself. So we said hello to the gent; he said hello and didn't linger long for he wanted to get to the lake to catch his breakfast. He was starving, so we said, "Well, we don't want to hold you up so go ahead of us, goodbye, see you at the lake."

He was a young guy, a lot younger than me and young enough to be my father-in laws grandson. I believe this might have been one of the last times I was blessed to hike with my father in-law into a high mountain lake. We live in Washington State in the Puget Sound area, sixty miles north of Seattle at the foothills of the Cascade Mountain range near Mount Baker which is an active volcano. His name is James; we've done quite a bit of hiking over the years. James is an avid fisherman, high lakes, or ones you can drive to he fishes them all including all the rivers in our area. He was a hunter for many years but he gave that up, and now just sticks with the rod and reel. He came here to Washington State with his family from North Carolina in the fifties with many other families mostly due to the abundance of work in the timber industry. He was a middle-schooler in the eighth grade, what you would call "genuine tar heel."

Back to our hike, James had been on a diet and just lost over thirty pounds to get in shape for this hike. He was a big man standing six foot four and weighing in at two hundred and thirty pounds. He was looking forward to retirement and it was right around the corner for him. He dreamed of fishing more and more and more. He owned an aluminum river sled-boat in which he used frequently to fish the rivers and lakes. He always loved to take friends and family fishing when he could. The Lord had blessed James with a wonderful wife, her name is Linda and she helped lead him to the Lord. He also had two daughters who are identical twins Jamie and Janet, I married Janet.

James was no stranger to hard work; he overcame many obstacles during his life. One of those obstacles was his education as he dropped out of school after eighth grade. This I learned from being teased for the way he spoke, the southern accent from his childhood home. Fortunately James possessed willpower and fortitude, he worked hard and learned how to break the bonds of poverty. He invested his earnings in retirement funds for he and Linda's future to prepare for retirement; he went back to school later in life and received a GED, which is equivalent to a high school diploma. James never had a son though he loved me as if I was his own. I looked up to him, my relationship with James was much more intimate compared to my biological father or stepfather combined.

James helped me with everything; he was always there when I needed a hand or guidance. I learned many lessons from him. We don't always realize at the moment when it happens but the things we teach someone or someone becomes a mentor for us, we teach or we learn, this is all from God. He has gifted each one for specific circumstances, moments in time in each one's life to minister to certain individuals that God brings across our path without our knowledge no plan of our own, just God working with our destiny. These things left a remarkable stain on my being, I remember every detail every moment, I will be able to be a conduit for someone else when its time. I will pass these truths down to another.

Here's the scenario: I was designed to be the perfect instrument for God to use, so James is able to accomplish God's perfect plan in him, likewise, James was perfectly suited and gifted to carry out God's plan, which was intended for the growth that would take place in my life. We both were specially gifted for this unique plan in each one of our lives, him for me, and me for him, intricately designed by God, woven together in one moment in time.

James began working in the shake mills after he quit school. At that time in the 1960s and '70s cedar was logged mostly for making shakes and shingles for roofing material and siding. There were quite a few mills in our little valley for men to make a good wage. James earned good money as a shake sawyer for not having much education. He would also install new roofs on houses when he could, he loved working with wood, he even had his own little wood shop, and he also loved building structures. I helped him with some of these projects. He helped me build two houses for my wife and I. He always wanted to help wherever he could. I recall one year we were installing a new composition roof on our little church, the steeple needed to be completely rebuilt so James volunteered to do it all by himself. We hired a crane to lift it off the church and into his truck and he drove it to his shop. I think it took about a week for him to restore it. He completely disassembled it, rebuilt it with new wood and shingles and reinstalled the bell, he was proud as a peacock when it was displayed back up on the church. I was impressed to say the least. We worked together on many projects during his time here on earth. When the timber industry fell apart due to environmental restrictions James went to work at both of the local oil refineries in our county. He moved up the ladder quickly and became a supervisor.

Sadly, I must say we received some horrible news one day. James had been having health issues and his doctor wasn't sure what was happening to James. So he sent James to a specialist at Virginia Mason Medical Center in Seattle. We were told James had ALS, Lou Gehrig's disease, we were crushed, and James was just sixty years young. The prognosis was bleak. The doctor told us he may have twelve to fourteen months to live. He had the most serious type and rarest. Some people can live as much as ten years after diagnosis a slow debilitating deterioration of their muscle and nerve function, but this was not what James had. His type would be quick, this news was deeply devastating.

James would be turning sixty-one shortly—sad news for his birthday. He was so looking forward, with anticipation to retirement. He and his wife Linda, my wife's mother, were planning to do some traveling; he wanted to go to Alaska to fish. Sadly, James went to be with the Lord the next year, two months short of his sixty second birthday. I find it troubling and difficult to understand this, God's plan in all this, did this have to be, was this God's providence? Did James fulfill God's assignment, how did James accomplish or finish the projects he was appointed to build here on earth? Did God's plan manifest and come to completion in the life of James? There is so much more he may have finished or accomplished for God if his life had been lengthened. We will never come to this knowledge, concerning birth, life, death, and time. My heart aches for those who were so special and dear to me. I live with anger for learning to let go of them but refusing to let go of the feelings of loss. But the truth is, it was their time, all planned in accordance with God's providence. I'm always given the same advice when I vent my frustration about providence. Man should not question God. Can I at least have a conversation with him? God's heart aches at the death of his saints just like ours. James followed Christ Jesus for many years. He served in his church as an elder doing God's work diligently always willing to do more, grateful and thankful for whom God created him to be. "Godliness with contentment is great gain" (1 Timothy 6:6).

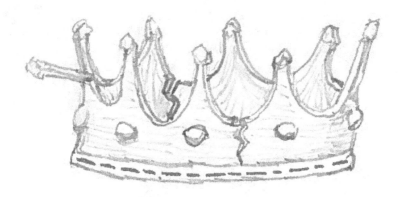

ECCLESIASTES

I wrote in a previous chapter about King Solomon and honing in on certain parts of his life and service to the Lord. Solomon was very successful in all his endeavors; he accomplished many wonderful and spectacular building projects for Israel. God blessed him with many riches for the kingdom and many allies to depend on. Solomon had some things that began to haunt him later in life, let's discuss a few. When a person reads through Ecclesiastes, he can sense Solomon's distress and despair. He seems to have lost his meaning and purpose in life. He is no longer familiar with his gifts or his unique specific purpose only he can do. He's confused and displays much anguish. His continence seems lowly; however, he continues to immerse himself in many projects testing the waters testing his mind and heart. Ultimately the conclusions and answers to this dilemma he's been searching for are out in the open, right in front of this poor old senile king. Sadly, he has been deceived by the one thing he wrote about and warned generations who would read his wisdom, the heart of man. The disease Solomon is suffering from is blossoming from his own seeds which he planted. Reading through Ecclesiastes you can sense his urgency. This man who years earlier owned a genuine humble heart, he wanted nothing more than to be a great leader for Israel. He asked for wisdom and discernment, a humble request coming from a newly crowned king. I go to the book of Ecclesiastes frequently, it is one of my favorites, mostly for I can relate to its substance, and examples of life.

This book illustrates many moments that are familiar. I, like Solomon become frustrated in the same manner and ask the same questions, why, what is there to gain from doing this or that, what do you want God what is your plan for me? What should I do, or where should I go, where should I put my energy and ability to work? What about the skills and talents you blessed me with, what resources will I need to become who you destined me to become, or is there a project you might be leading me to take on, who do I listen to, most often the one who answers my questions is my own heart. These are the struggles Solomon spoke about in Ecclesiastes. This book in some ways seems similar to a book of laments. This could be its label if one did not know better. Solomon lost his close fellowship with God do in part from the compromising of his virtues. He placed his energies into pleasure and sensualism and placed God behind these things. This is no different than what we do today in our secular world, pleasure before worship and devotion.

Perhaps Solomon recognized this and knew full well what he had done, but by then, it was too late and God had made his decision. That being said, I believe Solomon lamented his loss of closeness with God and he had no real solution to change the mind of God. He would learn to live with his mistakes. Praise God that we have his word and Jesus, and the Holy Ghost to guide us in these times of doubt and uncertainty. Our life struggles and goals and accomplishments parallel Solomon in that we fight the similar desires of the heart and wrestle with the lust of our eyes. Verses like "For there is a proper time and procedure for every matter, though a man's misery weighs heavy upon him" (Ecclesiastes 8:6). Even Solomon carried worry and anxiety as if he was carrying heavy stones on his back. Then chapter 6 verse 7: "All man's efforts are for his mouth yet his appetite is never satisfied." I wonder how many people who don't know God, who have never set their eyes upon this verse, who in their greed continue to relieve their need for acquiring wealth, if someone was to persuade them to help the needy with their resources their answer would be "when I win that lottery jackpot I can do so much more for people in need."

Look at verse 12: "For who knows what is good for man in life, during the few and meaningless days"; this is despair and hopelessness, sounds so familiar, are we not similar in our thoughts and feelings, is this the desperation of the heart? Then in chapter 7, Solomon speaks of death, I can't help but assume he may had considered suicide, possibly for a moment, just a thought, but read it (verses 1–2), "the day of death is better than the day of birth." "For death is the destiny of every man." Maybe he wasn't contemplating suicide but perhaps he was becoming old and tired and ready to throw in the towel once again lamenting.

And chapter 9 verse 5: "For the living know that they will die, but the dead know nothing, they have no further reward and even the memory of them is forgotten." Reward. What reward could Solomon be referring to? Also chapter 7 verse 14: "When times are good, be happy, but when times are bad, consider; God has made the one as well as the other. Therefore a man cannot discover anything about his future." This is a troubling observation, this statement seems as though it is fatalism, but in reality this is a solemn reminder God limits the information he gives to us for our own good and his providence.

In summary, Ecclesiastes can be and is still a great wealth of wisdom; even today, it speaks volumes about life and death.

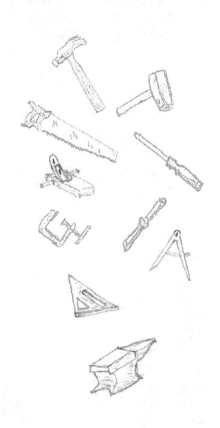

TOOLS

The tools God uses to build each one of his creations, they are not tangible instruments. Humans are intricately fashioned piece by piece to fit together, designed differently each for a certain application as David declared, "knit together in the secret place." Brilliantly put together to begin the purpose laid out for them. The tools God uses to build his creations are not tangible pieces made of iron or plastic, items that you can see or pick up with your hands. They are invisible, hidden, unknown. We often retaliate or squirm when he uses them on us. Among these tools we find patience; this is a hard one to swallow, I have no time to deal with this one, and I'm in a hurry I can't wait at all. The next one is; loss, this is ridiculous and miserable, I can't find a way to deal with this thing. Then we have rejection, I have no way to accept it. I will not! No solution for getting it back, we all have experienced it during some point in life. Then there is hopelessness; I always need to remind myself this type of thing is not going to happen no matter what I believe pessimism is the best medicine. Make no mistake these tools are painful. We try to be stoic, but we break down crying out to God, "Please this is to painful please stop." These growing pains are a normal part of his process, they are to be expected. Cry out to your God, if you must, he wants to hear your pleas; he cares deeply for you and wants to meet your deepest needs. Speak to him, share your fears with him; meet with him in your most secret place.

The most painful moments of being built, generally speaking are the most productive ones. Tools that may feel good are probably not tools God would use on us, but someone else's tools. God may take a lifetime to finish his work in you. Although along the way you are his instrument of purpose as well. You are not a clone and surely not a robot, but a living breathing creature working through your depravity focusing on sanctification and regeneration. He is compelled to change us into the children he longs for us to become. Perhaps it would profit our growth if he made our journey with fewer obstacles do you think? Not, we need them to strengthen our being. If we have to struggle in this sinful world, in order to become the creatures God intended for us to become, would these struggles and obstacles be necessary if there was no sin in the world? Does God use these same tools in heaven, or different ones? Maybe all things will be made proper and right, made to last for eternity, "he who is sitting on the throne said, I am making everything new!" (Revelation 21:5).

SIGNIFICANT

Significant moments, have you had one or two, or many in your life? Perhaps you have had none you can think of at this time? Or it is somewhat unclear to you what a significant moment really is. There can be different levels for everyone. People measure these things with similar barometers but can interpret them entirely different. Some of these significant moments God has planned for us include our family members, such as our spouse, our children, our parents and grandparents as well as our in-laws, and aunts, uncles, nieces, and nephews, also step-family members. All people in your life can be involved in significant moments in your life in accordance with God's providence. Demonstrating your gifts or skill at fatherhood can be a significant moment for you, or for your children, and be a positive or negative endeavor whichever you choose. So how do we define a significant moment? What classifies as one, what makes these blocks of time special or memorable good or bad? As we continue through our life journey will we be given revelation as part of our destiny, for each significant moment, in order for God to accomplish each bit of his work in our walk? Are these conditions used to influence our decision making process? Is it possible perhaps these moments in time; seconds, minutes, hours, days, weeks, and so on that take place are not always special or joyful. In fact they may be bad or sorrowful or dreadful. But they all have meaning, significant meaning.

There is always a lesson to learn among these pieces of significance. They should impact us enough in order to program our memories to keep a catalog to return to when needed, in order for our minds to refer to in part and parcel at a moment's request. On the contrary, this will help impact our character possibly for the better in a marvelous way. We are being transformed from the inside out by our God; always taking inventory of our situation namely our roll in God's providence. We should ask ourselves certain questions for example; are we fulfilling a role, or are we role playing, or is the role we are currently in God's role for us, or is it our own version of what we believe it to be? Was it conjured up from our own dreams and desires deep within our hearts and minds?

What does it cost to find out our significance? What must we do to know for sure, what must we pay for it, or is it free? How do we embrace it, our true and significant gift, what can we give to the potter? At any rate, significance, what does this mean? When you look back at your life whether you're a teen or young adult, middle aged or nearing retirement, or at the end holding on for dear life have you been significant? Perhaps you have discovered that you are in a significant moment? "I will lead the blind in paths they have not known. I will turn darkness into light before them, and make crooked things straight. These things I will do for them, and not forsake them" (Isaiah 42:16).

GIFTS

"For we are God's workmanship, created in Christ Jesus to do good works, which God prepared in advance for us to do" (Ephesians 2:10, NIV). Many people may not know the word; workmanship in Greek is a connotation that means "work of art"—this is so special. There is a specific task that only you can do, he created each one of us uniquely for a specific purpose. There's a calling, an adventure, a legacy meant for each one of us to leave. Even Jesus said, "You are worth more than many sparrows; the hairs of your head are all numbered." We have to be uniquely crafted and specially designed for our personal purpose for God, otherwise we would just be generic and vanilla, and there would be no individualism just humans. We would be insignificant people born into space and time randomly in a sea of people which outnumber the grains of sand on the beaches of this earth with no apparent differences, nothing to set us apart one from another. Are you hand crafted, are you a work of art, or are you invented? Which one are you?

DAMNED

Our benevolent God in his great providence has willed every person he creates to live in a holy relationship with him. Unfortunately, humans choose to live in hostility toward God. Calvinist would argue that those who abhor a relationship with God are created to be lost, however God is a God of love, this would be contrary to his character, and it would be despicable. People are damned for eternity for the simple reason the spirit cannot change their heart. The heart can be hard and calloused, unable for the spirit to break; it can't respond even if it feels the tug; the world has a great influence on the heart. The desire to find God is not there so they make a choice and are never aware they did. God does not predestine them to hell from before the day of their conception, though he has knowledge and data regarding every human beings heart.

Jesus states in Mathew 13, "The parable of the sower" that, unfortunately, the seed of salvation may fall on rocky ground or among thorns and thistles or on the side of the road where birds come and eat them, so is this grace left to fortune and chance? In John 6:65, Jesus also says no one can come to him only if the Father permits this. Clearly, this shows these people's hearts can be changed by the Holy Spirit and made able to accept the gift of grace and salvation only because of God's action. However, if God cannot change their heart, he leaves them in their sin, never overpowering their free will.

He is omnipotent and omniscience; he knows those who will follow him and those who will deny him. I say his heart aches for those who choose death over life. This is not predestination to be damned by God, unfortunately it is voluntary damnation. Committing one's self to hell and not being aware of it. The call of the spirit is universal so no one has an excuse. God wants all people to answer the call but tragically this will not happen. This is not God's perfect will for these souls, but it is part of his permissive will for he will never force anyone to choose him instead of other choices available to them. It's never easy to comprehend certain biblical truths or ideas however; there are many interpretations from different church denominations.

What it boils down to is this: God knows our hearts. God examines our hearts, and he chooses those God seeking hearts to be his children, those lost souls that are alive don't realize, they are really dead. "Praise be to the God and Father of our Lord Jesus Christ, who has blessed us in the heavenly realms with every spiritual blessing in Christ, for he chose us in him before the creation of the world to be holy and blameless in his sight. In love he predestined us to be adopted as his sons through Jesus Christ, in accordance with his pleasure and will to the praise of his glorious grace" (Ephesians 1:3–6).

SAMUEL ELI, HANNA

The account of Samuel is another fascinating story I enjoy reading it from time to time. There is a lot going on which we can apply to our own lives. Let's start with Eli the priest and his destiny. Unfortunately there was some depravity taking place regarding his leadership among the temple priest. His sons were part of this group—Hophni and Phinehas. These sons of Eli disregarded the temple protocol which required the meat to be boiled for the Passover in order to symbolize the freedom from bondage from the Egyptians. Eli's sons would take some meat by force and roast it for themselves which was forbidden. They also slept with the women who served at the entrance to the tent of meeting. Eli lost favor in the sight of the Lord to a great extent for being complacent about his son's actions. He would continue to warn them but he should have removed them from their positions in the priesthood. Eli also accused Hannah, Samuels mother, for coming to the temple to pray while she was intoxicated from beer and wine even though it was forbidden. If she was drunk he was required to remove her from the temple so once again he became complacent about the requirement and fortunately Hannah was not drunk she was just overwhelmed with grief and sorrow over her circumstances.

She was praying from her heart to the Lord. All Hannah wanted was to have children, this was very important, for being barren was considered a curse. Eli's actions are a good example of how far even the head priest had fallen from closeness to God. Eli let his son's actions sway his judgement. He put them before God. Eli's destiny is very ironic; He fell over while sitting in his chair and broke his neck because he was very large. This, more than likely is from indulging, fattening himself and his sons on the choice meats taken from the Lord (1 Samuel 2:29–33). God blessed the house of Hannah but cursed the house of Eli. Samuel on the other hand turned out to be completely different than Eli and his sons even though he served alongside them. His example was holy continence with a spirit compelled to serve God whole heartedly. I'm in awe when I read through these texts, mostly from the contrast of the characters. Hannah was more familiar with and in touch with the most important parts in that she demonstrated great faith toward God. Faith releases the believer to take great risks.

She dedicated her firstborn to the service of God, and he blessed her for this commitment and devotion. She had been intensely taunted and abused at the hands of her rival wife but she showed perseverance. One can see the Lords purposes after reading these scriptures. These scriptures say the Lord closed Hannah's womb. He was working his plan all along for he knew she had a pure and loving heart. He caused this in order for her to dedicate her firstborn for he knew it to be Samuel, and Samuel was the one he had purposed to anoint the first two kings of the nation Israel. He already planned this from eternity beginning; interesting to note even though Samuel refused to follow in the wicked examples Eli and his sons exhibited when he became old and beyond years, he passed his leadership onto his sons, Joel and Abijah, who were just as wicked as Eli and his sons. Samuel obviously did not take heed to the actions Eli used in raising his sons for they were passed down to Samuel's. One man's cup of righteousness and holiness does not always runneth over on to his children. This story features people who lived in the same community but each had very different destinies, Hannah lived longer and was blessed with many more sons and daughters but Eli and his sons chose a dreadful road which led to death for their destiny. They were unrepentant, showing only gluttony and selfishness. After Samuel gave his report to Eli which he received from God about Eli's destiny for his wickedness, Eli's response: "He is the Lord let him do what seems best." Eli should have gotten down on his knees and repented and begged for mercy but he was too proud. Could it be possible that God hardened the hearts of Eli and his sons? Scripture does say it was God's will to put them to death (1 Samuel 2:25).

Eli knew his destiny and chose to accept it; instead he might have been able to persuade God to dispense mercy rather than wrath. If only he would have walked in a different direction one that leads straight to God. His entire family suffered the penalty for his complacency. Was this his purpose in life; was this what he was created for? Samuel on the other hand chose the better road, even though, he was blessed to talk to God in the first person, just like Eli once did I assume. This is a much-needed benefit there is no second guessing. We don't have this luxury today. I have never heard a sermon which focuses and examines the parts and people who seem to be insignificant in the beginning chapters of 1 Samuel. My hope is to illustrate the similarities that will encourage us to be who God created us to be. First, we must get to know him second, discover his reason for crafting his children and third, pour our heart out to him, and forth, love him and worship him with authenticity. "Trust in the Lord with all your heart and lean not on your own understanding; in all your ways acknowledge him, and he will make your paths straight" (Proverbs 3:5–6).

HEARTS

God can soften the heart of anyone if he so chooses. However, he has demonstrated through many examples in scriptures, where he may harden some people's hearts as well. The intense heat from a fiery furnace is able to melt wax and harden clay. In contrast this is a great example of the omnipotence and providence of God. This is very mysterious; I continue to apply my mind, in order to somehow wrap it around this theological concept. Why some people have hearts that may be pliable and workable, easy to soften by the spirits call. And some people with hearts of stone cannot respond to or recognize his presence tugging at their soul. And then after a certain amount of time we read in scripture the Lord leaves them in their sin and may send a stumbling block for these individuals who, have been living with hardened hearts for a long time.

Some biblical experts may advocate this is evidence suggesting God has destined these people for damnation; they also suggest he needed to be more patient with these people; nevertheless God does know all things from beginning to end. I believe these are lost souls, and God is entirely aware of this fact. He also knows their destiny as they will never respond to the spirits call, even though God could over power their will, he will not, he leaves them to make their own choice even if they choose death. These people will never let the Holy Spirit into their being; they are immune to the spirits refining fire. Like clay in the hands of a potter they cannot be molded, like iron in the hands of a blacksmith they cannot be shaped and pounded into anything useful, like wood in the hands of a carpenter there is no tools which will trim them or sand the rough edges smooth, they would sink to the bottom of the ocean with no need of a millstone tied around their neck for they are to heavy and hard and dense, a cold stone. God can do nothing to change their destiny or their choice.

Remember, God has divine authority; he has the legal and moral right to carry out his will according to his providence. He is not obligated to give life to any of these individuals who have rejected him. I know this is a hard pill to swallow for some folks, but in reality scripture is clear not everyone will be saved. Can we discover other truths in this area, what else is there to dig up regarding our ultimate God given gift? "There is a way that seems right to a man, but in the end it leads to death. Even in laughter the heart may ache, and joy may end in grief. The faithless will be fully repaid for their ways, and the good man rewarded for his. A simple man believes anything, but a prudent man gives thought to his steps" (Proverbs 14:12–15).

ROE V. WADE

MURDERED PEOPLE

Generally speaking, if we believe every human being is created for a unique purpose one in which they are not just ordinary but meant for some type of significance, foreordained from eternity beginning, saved and unsaved chosen and damned each one with a definitive blueprint from God for their life, the magnitude of people who have been killed from the beginning of time is huge. Where does this leave these people, was their extermination God's plan for them? How is this, their destiny, those who fell prey to dictators and haters of all nationalities and religions of the world, those who were tortured and slain, men women and innocent babies, children and the unborn. I realize a good portion of these were pagan nations apposing God and the nation Israel, however, a large multitude of these people were good and moral people who worshiped Yahweh. How does this fit into God's plan, are they collateral damage? Why was it his will for them to be doomed to this destiny? We can go back even before the scriptures were penned and see this pattern. Evil men do dastardly deeds, things to other men, human beings. God did allow the annihilation of the foreign nations in the biblical record wiping out an unimaginable number of men and women and children mostly due to their worship of false gods, and for their wickedness.

So what do we do with all the innocent souls who lost their lives, what category do we put them in, those who were murdered by the Chinese or Stalin or Hitler, how was this part of God's plan? Was this his perfect will or permissive will? Similar to the story of Job in content so are the stories of these people. These losses are written on the hearts of their dear families causing pain and agony for many people. Sin is the root and cause, though it is God using all this tragedy for his purpose. Should we ask these questions, or spend considerable thought on such issues, or are they off limits all together? I am certain we should not forget or bury these horrendous atrocities but put them in a place where they will always be a reminder of the sin which displaces us from communion with our God. I believe once again God wants his children to pour their hearts out to him; he knows our sorrow and pain and wants nothing better than to hold us and comfort us. "Praise be to the God and Father of our Lord Jesus Christ, the Father of compassion and the God of all comfort, who comforts us in all our troubles, so that we can comfort those in any trouble with the comfort we ourselves have received from God" (2 Corinthians 1:3–4).

TRADES

Earlier in this book, I mentioned a little about my own career path and the amount of searching I exercised. I was hoping to find my niche, thinking and convinced I knew what the best vocation was for my life. I never once gave any thought to what I might have been created to be or do. I never, not once asked God not once. I always had the idea it was my responsibility to search and discover my profession. Here is a list of all the occupations I participated in from childhood to adult; lawn boy, gofer for my stepfather, he was a plumber, ditch digger, laborer for a local building contractor, worked for a logging company, digging fire trail cleaning brush and debris out of creeks, cleaning culverts, setting chokers on a logging crew, operating logging equipment, which includes dozers, skidders and log loaders for loading log trucks. I also cut timber with a chain saw (timber faller) cutting trees, making them into logs to be milled into dimensional lumber, ironically I also worked at various lumber mills. I also am a journeymen tree trimmer; this involves climbing trees as well as operating a bucket truck to trim tree branches away from electrical power lines. My wife and I have done property management and land development; I've been a draftsman mechanical and architectural. I also worked for an asphalt company part-time. I worked for the National Park Service and the Forestry Department. I worked for a milk and ice cream company operating packaging and bottling machines.

I worked in the heating and air conditioning industry installing new equipment in commercial and residential buildings. I worked as a garbage man throwing cans into a garbage truck and driving one. I've also been a home builder, I worked for a while as a handyman, and currently I have been in the wastewater business, I have an equivalent to a master's degree in wastewater biology and chemistry. I oversee the process and manage a one-hundred-million dollar treatment facility. I have no idea whether these occupations were in God's plan for me however, in every instance I prayed, God please give me this job, he did answer me, sometimes he made it possible for me to take the job but, sometimes he also closed the doors. He very well might have been manipulating the circumstances for his plans.

This is conceivable, perhaps his plan all along has been to saturate my being with many opportunities to, learn and master different skills, in order to gain versatility, not to confuse me but on the contrary; he is now able to use me in many capacities. This has been very frustrating for me, though I know I'm not the only one among millions who are or have anguished because of this. I have heard other people share their experiences with me and most have come to similar conclusions believing and giving up completely on finding their true purpose and giftedness, as well as their unique destiny or God given skills or vocation. So as I've said, this isn't entirely a negative position. Looking back, reviewing my occupational history, I can pick out moments in which I did make an impact or witness in someone else's life. Could it be, maybe I fulfilled a portion of the purpose God planned for me, even though I struggled during these moments, self-motivated to discover my destiny time after time I became disappointed; finally, my eyes have been opened after all these years, and now I realize what I need to do to find my gift and unique purpose, and you can too.

Make your relationship with God deeper, put him first. We can resist sin the spirit is willing to help you. Enoch was taken away because he put sin away, and he was privileged to see the deeper things of the Lord. Then you will find who you are who God planned you to be, don't lose hope, it may take your whole life to know for sure exactly what you are created to be. We are privileged ever more than Enoch I believe. We are filled with the Holy Spirit, who enables us to put away sin; we can get closer to our God and see the workmanship of our being. You're a work of art, specially crafted unique, one of a kind, find your calling discover your gifted abilities. Pursue that profession or trade, enterprise, field, livelihood start your adventure today. "I will instruct you and teach you in the way you should go; I will council you and watch over you" (Psalms 32:8).

BORN TO DIE

I saved this story for the end of this book. I hope this will encourage and comfort people rather than be a downer. My daughter has some high school friends who now are married; they have been out of school for seven years. They gave birth to twins six months ago, a boy and a girl; they were premature. They each weighed barely two pounds. The little girl developed an infection, which turned from staff to mersa, and she passed away at only two months old. I have never been burned in this furnace of agony these parents are in right now; I don't know what to make of this dilemma. Is this a curse? Is it bad luck, or what other power could do such a thing to this young, newlywed couple? I can't fathom the emotions they must be carrying at this moment. It will be difficult to say the least for them to endure this tragedy if they are Christians but what if they are not, their young marriage will be a struggle without God.

To lose a child at any age is horrific, but to lose a baby who is premature where they only live for a few months would be devastating. Imagine the stress and anxiety of the unknown saturating these new parents who haven't been married long, indescribable. I know this happens every day all around the world although when it happens so close to home a person can't help but feel the pain of this young family. This significant moment in time will be with them forever; it may haunt their union forever. Hopefully, they can overcome this and not let it tear them apart. I'm sure it is different for losing an infant, wondering, never able to see that child grow or hear them laugh or smile, or watching them grow into a child then an adolescent to a teen and becoming an adult. They will miss out on many special moments, how can this be, what plan or purpose can be achieved from all this? Is this the destiny of this innocent precious baby, how could anything good come of this? X is good if X = the will of God.

The baby twin boy who is healthy and growing, what will his mother and father say to him later in his life, when he is old enough to understand, concerning his lost sibling? Why has this little girl been taken away and the little boy not? Is it healthy to ask these questions? Can we be patient, can we be able to wait until the day God reveals these unknowns to us. The little boy will ask these same questions someday. He may have no second thoughts about the matter, even though his parents needed strength to carry on, he might understand later in life, the load his mother and father carried during this time of loss and mourning. God feels the hurt just as we do; he laments with us, he can be trusted with our children. Often it's difficult to believe anything good will come from these situations, it is within God's purpose to use these tribulations to build resilience into us, this is his sovereignty at work; He is in control in every crisis that occurs. All through this book I've touched on certain real life examples and struggles from people of the Bible and people who have made an impact in my journey. I hope to gain some insight if any on the workmanship of our person by the great craftsman. There are no easy answers for us to fall back on, to settle our emotions our plans, our purposes, our destiny. However we can take comfort in knowing our time here on earth is preplanned. Each one of us is one piece of a big jigsaw puzzle, each is unique and fits into the spot specific to its design, no other piece will fit in yours, God has uniquely prepared this spot for you his precious child "the Lord is close to the broken hearted and saves those who are crushed in spirit" (Psalms 34:18).

"And we know that in all things God works for the good of those who love him, who have been called according to his purpose" (Romans 8:28).

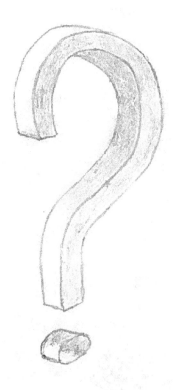

LIVE FOR SOMETHING

Do you live for something? Do you live for playing golf? Do you live for money? Do you live for attaining wealth? Do you live for football? Do you live for cars? Do you live for partying? Do you live for alcohol? Do you live for drugs? Do you live for sex? Do you live for animals? Do you live for saving the earth? Do you live for work? Do you live for competition? Do you live for food? Do you live for physical fitness? Do you live to rule? Do you live to serve? Do you live to love? Do you live to hate? Do you live to kill? Do you live to save lives? Do you live for yourself? Do you live for others? Do you live for changing the world? Do you live for making the world better? Do you live for creating hurt and chaos and damage? Do you live for your children? Do you live for your spouse? Do you live for your neighbor? Do you live for the sick? Do you live for prisoners? Do you live for orphans? Do you live for the poor? Do you live for the widows? Do you live for yard sales? Do you live for acquiring things? Do you live for revenge? Do you live for fighting? Do you live for peace? Do you live for war? Do you live for showing mercy and forgiveness? Do you live for a good cause? Do you live for Buddha? Do you live for Allah? Do you live for your church? Do you live for God? Do you live for Jesus Christ? What do you live for?

Live to be filled with the Holy Ghost.

Live to be like Jesus.

Live to glorify God.

CONCLUSION

By now, you are more than likely wondering, *Where will I go from here?* Your anxiousness has increased rather than decreased, saying to yourself under your breath, "I'm sure glad God has been more generous to me as far as revealing more of my crafted abilities than he's been to this guy." I've determined in my study of these issues; we may explore these unknown divine designed products and we should, God wants wholeheartedly for each one of his children to be searching continually for his grand plan for our life, our abilities, our training, our talents, our experiences, in order to discover parts of our uniqueness or all of it. God has already given us the perfect set of skills we need. My hope is this book gives each person insight into the one and only place to find their true self, the one of a kind creature. You were hand crafted to be a workmanship made for his purpose and glory only, not some glamorous dream you conjured up as a child, not the job you wanted when you finished college because it pays a six-figure salary—no, the only thing that truly matters most is his plan for you. Time is of the essence; we have no time to sit and smell the roses, now is the time. Our lives are but a breath in light of eternity; we are nothing; the time is now. It's time to execute the commands of Jesus. God says, "I desire obedience not sacrifices"; therefore, let us be found doing our Lord's work unto death or until his return, whichever comes first. Why would we choose to linger any longer in the flesh, or wallow in our selfishness, and dabble in worldly passions? God wants us now, not just part, but all of our person; he wants it all, complete abandonment. Jesus wants our every second. We are always reluctant to let go of our dreams, and we find it difficult to imagine God not giving each of us what we want. The truth is yes, he may give you what you want; he won't force you or twist your arm to do what he wants you to do. He will not stop you from pursuing your dreams or your interest. There are no words which are sufficient to describe the true discovery of one's fulfillment and happiness which come from a life completely devoted to serving our lord. Someday from now, when you are at the end of your life: will you have any regrets, or will you be waiting in joyful anticipation to stand face to face with Jesus whom you served unselfishly on earth? "The King of Glory."

The great preacher Charles Spurgeon once said, "You may fear that the Lord has passed you by, but it is not so; he who counts the stars in the sky, and calls them by name, is in no danger of forgetting his own children. He knows your case as thoroughly as if you were the only creature he ever made, or the only saint he ever loved, approach him and be at peace."

FURTHER INSIGHT
AND ADDITIONAL
OBSERVATIONS

The power of resentment: it will blind whoever embraces it. Chained for a lifetime are those who harbor it. Like a ball and chain locked to your ankle, sadly, most people think nothing of this at all; they give it no second thought. They may very well be comfortable pulling and jerking this extra weight, convinced that this is okay. This is somewhat similar to having an extra bag to carry and check at the airport; they know it to be burdensome packing around this extra weight; nevertheless, they are convinced it is essential, and they need it to function every day of their life.

Resentment holds us hostage, hostage to our own view and perception of ourselves. Over time, this thing will spill over into all avenues of our lives. We begin to become more and more self-serving and angry for the things we never received, or the places we believed we should have reached or found, or dreams which never came to pass and we feel slighted or mistreated; we begin to feel as if we have no worth. Ultimately, this position will have a huge effect on the way we view ourselves, our life, and our existence.

When I was a little boy, I knew nothing of resentment, even though I practiced it for those first years; only until I became old enough to understand a bit of this principle was I able to really embrace it. I was a stepchild, and I struggled to understand why this was. I saw my friends and their families and the wholeness they experienced, and this motivated my resentment even more.

This motivation did blossom into solid positive goals, which I promised myself to accomplish.

I vowed to myself to strive for a more positive environment if I was blessed with a family. I also would make this vow to God and whoever I would marry and to our children as well, and not to embrace divorce as a default if things became tough. Sadly, the resentment still lingers in the shadows. First and foremost, a person has to identify the cause of the resentment before they can deal with it. There may be many issues which are fueling resentment. Where does this thing come from? Should this be a natural emotion? What about Christians? Are they immune from this handicap? My perception and experience with this dilemma tells me that most people, those who are not Christians, most often believe Christians view themselves as being perfect and holy and well protected from the rest of civilization and its shortfalls. However, this is not the case. Christians have a much more difficult row to hoe in my opinion. I believe their struggle is much more intense, at least from my angle of sight. I am a Christian, so I do have a first-person perspective. Resentment, this feeling or emotion, whatever you want to call it, is real. And Christians are just ordinary people, as well as those who are not, but Christians choose a different mechanism, a different mode of operation, to latch onto during these times, so to speak.

Looking back now, I can see much clearer what took place. From the moment we are able to think and reason, we begin to develop this hope and imagery of being the apple of someone, or anyone's eye, wanting to be loved more than everyone. We begin to use comparisons to calculate our thoughts and train our minds. This can be very dangerous because no two people are the same, or in the same, situation. Even so, we conclude that we deserve better or deserve at least what the other fellow has. How silly are we humans, even Christians will covet non-Christian's circumstances and their lifestyles, as well as their possessions; this will begin to fan the little flame of resentment until it is a raging inferno hot and bright in their heart. Resentment is a poison that will kill you instantly if you drink it; don't drink it; give it to the cupbearer to sip.

He will never let his children be poisoned for we are the apple of his eye! Who is this cupbearer? The one and only Jesus the Nazarene, the Galilean, the Jew our God!

Do you harbor resentment for specific elements, such as broken dreams and goals, which never came to fruition in your life? Resentment will manipulate you; it will hold you hostage; it will keep you locked in a dungeon for years. How will we keep from cultivating it? What plants the seed in our mind? What fertilizes it? Where does it begin to grow and mature?

Perhaps you are resentful toward your mother, father, or both? Maybe one or both of them were alcoholics or drug users. Or they may have been abusive to you as a child. Perhaps you had a sibling who was their favorite, and it was obvious. Do you hold unto resentment in your heart in part for being a stepchild? You may have a stepmother or stepfather who brought their children into your family, and you always got shortchanged or the raw end of the stick?

Suppose you're resentful because you have a child who is rebellious and in trouble all the time or a drug user or in and out of jail. Or you may be raising a child who has special needs or is handicapped because of a tragic, unfortunate accident which has overwhelmed you to the point that you don't know who or where to turn. Maybe your son or daughter told you they were gay. Or suppose your spouse came to you and told you they were leaving and demanded a divorce. Perhaps you are a widow, or a widower, and you are left alone to raise your children by yourself, or maybe you lost a child to a terminal disease, or you are the only one caring for your aging parents. Suppose you were grieving because your spouse committed suicide, or you are devastated from your child committing suicide. Perhaps you have a disease or you're a handicap, and lastly, you could be resentful from looking back at your life and you see where you came from and where you are now, and you're just disgusted at how it all turned out.

Resentment fuels hate and the strong emotion of entitlement. Sooner or later, self-pity becomes common place; the "I deserve to have this" or "I deserve to be treated better"—these declarations ultimately will be the vehicles that will change our character and end up brainwashing our mind.

We find ourselves always turning to the hate mechanism when we encounter different situations, as we move through life. This doesn't have to be this way; don't be too hard on yourself. I have been a prisoner to resentment many times in my life. For some strange reason, it seems as though it may be a default mechanism in our genetic makeup, but it is just our fallen state. How many times do we have to be let down or fall short or not achieve that for which we have been striving for until we give up?

Unfortunately, we give in to disappointment, which leads us down the path to resentment. Just for the record, I believe a good portion of the moments I exercised resentment was meant to be aimed at God, rather than pointed at the people or circumstances that instigated my resentment. At times, I have found it frustrating to embrace my lot in life, even though it is what the Lord mapped out for me. Should we fail to remember what it says in scripture regarding the potter and the clay?

I have mentioned many scenarios in these last paragraphs, and there are many more; however, I believe you get the point. Now then, we all are prisoners, though we don't have to be. We need hope, and we have this in what Jesus accomplished for us, but in order to train our mind, we have some things to do as well.

We have hope, but sometimes we need inspiration and promises to ease our conscience and our minds. Here is a compilation of scriptures I have put together, which I believe will emulate these two positive things. I hope and pray you will be inspired.

And do not be conformed to this world, but be transformed by the renewing of your mind, that you may prove what the will of God is, that which is good and acceptable and perfect. (Romans 12:2)

> And the peace of God, which surpasses all understanding, will guard your hearts and your minds in Christ Jesus. (Philippians 4:7)

> Consider it pure joy, my brethren, when you encounter various trials. (James 1:2)

> Knowing that the testing of your faith produces endurance. (James 1:3)

Do not fear what you are about to suffer. Behold, the devil is about to cast some of you into prison, that you may be tested, and you will have tribulation ten days. Be faithful unto death, and I will give you the crown of life. (Revelation 2:10)

Rest in the Lord and wait patiently for Him. Don't be envious of evil men who prosper. For the wicked will be destroyed, do not be angry or worry but forsake wrath; this leads only to evil and they who are evil will be cut off. But those who wait for the Lord will inherit the land. (Psalms 37:7,8,9)

Blessed is a man who perseveres under trial; for once he has been approved, he will receive the crown of life which the Lord has promised to those who love him. (James 1:12).

We can rejoice, too, when we run into problems and trials for we know that they are good for us-they help us learn to be patient. And patience develops strength of character in us and helps us trust God more each time we use it until finally our hope and faith are strong and steady. (Romans 5:3,4)

Behold, we count those blessed who endured. You have heard of the endurance of Job and have seen the outcome of the Lord's dealings, that the Lord is full of compassion and is merciful. (James 5:11).

God has made an everlasting covenant with me; his agreement is eternal, final, sealed. He will constantly look after my safety and success. (2 Samuel 23:5).

He forgives all our sins and heals all our diseases. (Psalms 103:3)

Just as a father has compassion on his children, So the Lord has compassion on those who fear him. (Psalms 103:13)

Know that the Lord himself is God; it is He who has made us, and not we ourselves; we are his people and the sheep of his pasture. (Psalms 100:3)

Train up a child in the way he should go, and when he is old, he will not depart from it. (Proverbs 22:6)

Let your way of life be free from the love of money, being content with what you have; for he himself has said, "I will never desert you, nor will I ever forsake you. (Hebrews 13:5)

Come to me all who are weary and heavy-laden, and I will give you rest. Take my yoke upon you, and learn from me, for I am gentle and humble in heart; and you shall find rest for your souls. For my yoke is easy, and my burden is light. (Matthew 11:28–30)

Whoever keeps doing the will of God will live forever. (1 John 2:17)

Whatsoever we ask, we receive from him, because we keep his commandments, and do those things that are pleasing in his sight. (1 John 3:22)

All who listen to my instructions and follow them are wise, like a man who builds his house on the rock. (Matthew 7:24)

Be strong and let your heart take courage, all you who hope in the Lord. (Psalm 31:24)

The righteous shall move onward and forward; those with pure hearts shall become stronger and stronger. (Job 17:9)

He is a rewarder of them that diligently seek him. (Hebrews 11:6)

Draw near to God and he will draw near to you. (James 4:8)

For it is God at work in you, both to will and to work for his good pleasure. (Philippians 2:13)

For we are his workmanship, created in Christ Jesus for good works, which God prepared beforehand, that we should walk in them. (Ephesians 2:10)

And if you ask me anything in my name, I will do it. If you love me you will keep my commandments. (John 14:14,15)

And all things you ask in prayer, believing, you shall receive. (Matthew 21:22)

Though my father and mother forsake me, but the Lord will take me up. (Psalms 27:10)

Precious in the sight of the Lord is the death of his saints. (Psalms 116:15)

The Lord is near to the brokenhearted and he saves those who are crushed in spirit. (Psalms 34:18)

Let all the earth fear the Lord. (Psalms 33:8)

Behold the eye of the Lord is on those who fear him, on those who hope for his loving-kindness. (Psalms 33:18)

INDEX

Scripture References

Joshua 9:26–27
2 Samuel 11

Quotes Taken From

Dietrich Bonhoeffer
John Calvin
Martin Luther
Jonathon Edwards
Charles Spurgeon
Abraham Lincoln
James M. Grier
Switchfoot
Sylvester Stallone
Rocky 4
Joel Osteen
C. S. Lewis
Bob Barker
Saint Augustine
William Cary
Calvin Miller

NOTES

NOTES

NOTES

ABOUT THE AUTHOR

David C. Schorno has found himself working in many vocations during his life journey, hoping to discover his genuine one-of-a-kind gift or craft, which the great designer blessed him with. David lives in the Pacific Northwest sixty miles north of Seattle with his wife Janet of thirty-five years and their daughter Kristen where they have been serving the Lord together, teaching Sunday school and serving in church leadership roles for their entire married life. This is David's first book as a novice writer.

CPSIA information can be obtained
at www.ICGtesting.com
Printed in the USA
JSHW050234250222
23319JS00001B/32